AF325004

Essays in the History of Liberty

Essays in the History of Liberty:
SEAVER INSTITUTE LECTURES AT THE HUNTINGTON LIBRARY

1988

THE HENRY E. HUNTINGTON LIBRARY
SAN MARINO, CALIFORNIA

Copyright 1988 by the Huntington Library and Art Gallery

ISBN 0-87328-126-8

Printed in the United States of America

Library of Congress Number: 88-23638

CONTENTS

CONTRIBUTORS

Michael Les Benedict is presently professor at The Ohio State University, where he specializes in American legal and constitutional history. He is author of several books and articles on the politics and law of the Civil War and Reconstruction period. He has also published articles on the history of civil liberty, and is presently preparing a history of American civil rights and liberties. He is the author of *Civil Rights and Civil Liberties* (Washington, D.C., 1987) in the American Historical Association's series, *Bicentennial Essays on the Constitution*.

Don E. Fehrenbacher, Professor of History Emeritus at Stanford University, was the Huntington-Seaver Fellow in 1985-86. His most recent book is *Lincoln in Text and Context*.

Stanley I. Kutler is the E. Gordon Fox Professor of American Institutions and Professor of Law at the University of Wisconsin. His most recent book, *The American Inquisition: Justice and Injustice in the Cold War* (1982), received the American Bar Association's Silver Gavel Award. His new book, *The Age of Watergate*, will be published in 1989.

James M. McPherson, Edwards Professor of American History at Princeton University, is the author of many books on the Civil War period including *Battle Cry of Freedom: The Civil War Era*.

John Phillip Reid is professor of law at the New York University School of Law and the author of many books and articles in the fields of constitutional history of the American Revolution and law in the American westward movement. Among his recent books are *The Concept of Liberty in the Age of the American Revolution* and *Law For The Elephant: Property and Social Behavior on the Overland Trail*.

Harry N. Scheiber is professor of law at the University of California, Berkeley, and the author of many books and articles on law in society, including *Law in American History*.

INTRODUCTION

The essays in this volume were presented as a series of lectures at the Huntington Library during the past three years. The authors, distinguished scholars all, were invited to think about the history of liberty in American life and draft an essay on an aspect of it that would be of interest to an intelligent general public. The result of the Huntington's request for such essays has proven most rewarding indeed. The authors have dealt with topics so diverse as Lincoln, the law, religion, and race. The essays make excellent reading because they are the work of informed minds and because they are evocative. They challenge the reader to think about a subject that will always be with us—the nature and boundaries of the government in dealing with the lives of its citizens.

These essays were made possible by a grant from the Seaver Institute, which was established by Frank L. Seaver, a noted southern California industrialist. Frank L. Seaver had a deep concern about the continued economic growth of the United States in an environment that afforded the greatest possible personal liberty of the individual. He believed that personal liberty in its widest possible sense was essential to the health of this nation. The Seaver Institute has concentrated most of its efforts in the field of science and with the ramifications of scientific change in our society. These essays reflect a continuing debate about the nature of liberty in a modernizing scientific nation that emerged from colonialism in the eighteenth century and became the dominant world power in the twentieth.

It is especially appropriate that the essays were given as lectures at the Huntington Library. The founder of the Library, Henry Edwards Huntington, who shared many of the values of Frank L. Seaver, established the Library as a place to study the Anglo-American past to better understand our society in all its complexity. These lectures contribute to disseminating contemporary debate on a significant subject integral to his ideas about a research facility.

The Huntington Library gratefully acknowledges the generous gift of the Frank L. Seaver Institute that made these essays and their publication possible.

Martin Ridge
Head of Research, Huntington Library

Liberty and the Original Understanding

by John Phillip Reid

There is an apparent inconsistency in contemporary historical scholarship. At a time when a reviewer for the *New York Times* reports that historians have "proscribed the constitution as a topic of investigation" and that the study of history itself is perceived in the academy as becoming increasingly irrelevant,[1] the perception that history can be relevant has been growing in the market place of the law. This trend is not limited exclusively to constitutional litigation, but it is in constitutional law that the craft of history has become the most marked as a tool of advocacy. A measure of this development can be taken by noting that the use and usefulness of history in constitutional interpretation is a topic currently being debated in hundreds of pages of our law reviews. The debate, a recent participant observed, concerns "a question so abstract that those who focus on it have come to call themselves theorists"[2]—a term not often applied to lawyers. We may wonder if the matter in dispute would be better described as false history, for when lawyers ask the "original intent" of the framers of the Constitution, Bill of Rights, or Fourteenth Amendment, they often seek answers to questions about which the framers never thought, as they pose issues which the framers could not have comprehended. For that reason, it is sometimes contended, the role of history in constitutional advocacy should be confined to the broader, more easily answered historical questions. For example: whereas history cannot tell our judges what the framers thought about released time, the constitutional "privacy" of bath houses, or public payments for abortions, history is equipped to tell us what the framers meant by "representation," "government by consent," the right to trial by jury, and the power of taxation. An instance of a broad, researchable, "answerable" concept from the age of the founding of the republic is the concept of liberty.

We may be certain that we can reconstruct much of the eighteenth-century meaning of liberty, and we may also be certain that the founders felt that they were motivated by a desire to perpetuate liberty throughout the land. It might follow, then, that the concept of liberty could be a reliable guide for lawyers and judges interpreting the documents and applying the principles that the founders left us as their legacy.[3] But does it follow? We and the English-speaking people of the eighteenth century share the same word—liberty—but do we share the same idea? Is our understanding that the framers were committed to liberty of much use if their concept of liberty is no longer our concept?

There are many differences between the framers' "liberty" and our "liberty," and one of the most striking is the fact that had there been a written constitution and a supreme court in the eighteenth century, the word liberty would have been one of the most utilized normative concepts employed in constitutional interpretation. Liberty then would have been as potent as "due process of law" and "equal protection" have been in the twentieth century.[4] The reason we may make that guess is because of a second striking difference between then and now. It is the remarkable charm that the word "liberty" once held for the English-speaking people.

In the eighteenth-century vocabulary of Anglo-American politics and law no other term invoked more emotion than liberty. "There is not a word," Richard Price insisted, "which expresses so much of what is important and excellent."[5] Liberty may well have been the most trenchant word in the eighteenth-century English language. "There is," a British writer observed in 1776, "an enchantment in the sound of *liberty, free, self-governed*, and the like."[6] In the eighteenth century the concept of liberty was more than the sum of all its elements—the other sides of licentiousness and slavery, the rule of law, security of property, and principles of the constitution. It was also rhetoric, a way of arguing, of urging action, and of audience expectation. The rhetoric of liberty, so familiar, so anticipated, so persuasive because it was shared by all literate English-speaking people, was a potent force in eighteenth-century politics and constitutional debate.[7] It helped to set not only the tone of forensic exchange but also the political programs that men would initiate.

The coming of the American Revolution provided a great theater for the rhetoric of liberty. People on both sides of the controversy employed the language of liberty as a form of shorthand or code of cherished beliefs with which to argue, persuade, and motivate. Opponents could be condemned and allies praised by selecting the familiar, taught expression, hoping to provoke predictable reaction with charged meanings, conditioned prejudices, and historical fears. *Brutus* knew the right words to use when telling Virginians that tories were the "degenerate tools of lawless power" and whigs the "upright sons of constitutional liberty."[8] Today, *Brutus*'s words appear to be political bombast. In the eighteenth century they said more than that opponents were wicked and friends good. They elicited responses to arbitrariness, prerogativism, rule of law, restraint upon government, and constitutionalism.

Well should the British tingle to the word liberty, for liberty and the British were wed. It was liberty that gave the English, Scots, Welsh, and Americans as a people their uniqueness and their pride. Great Britain, after all, was "a land, wherein liberty is supposed to have fixed her favourite residence."[9] It was not only "the peculiar lot of Great Britain to have liberty, and the blessings deriving from it, to take up their abode with her,"[10] but "the History of England," was "the History of *Liberty*"[11] and "civil liberty" was "the second nature of Englishmen."[12] Indeed, Great Britain was "truly stiled, *the land of liberty*. Its subjects, from the mildness of its laws and the happiness of its religion, are blest beyond any other nation."[13]

The point was hardly subtle. The British were not only blessed, they were best, and it was because they were blessed that they were best. In their own estimation the British were the finest people on earth, the most honest, cheerful, compassionate, and hearty, eating the best roast beef, drinking the best water, and living the best lives. Their soldiers were invincible, their sailors "the bravest and honestest the World can boast of."[14] They were also the least oppressed, perhaps the only nation that did not know tyranny, living under a government *"founded on the* Principles of Liberty, by a WISE, a FREE, and BRAVE PEOPLE."[15]

The British were not vain about their race. They did not claim that they were naturally the world's best people, that they possessed inherent qualities that other nationalities lacked. It was liberty that made them best.[16] Because the argument is no longer familiar, it is worth quoting a typical instance of the boast so that its range and extent may not be underestimated.

[T]he English Character has acquired a vigour and a manliness from the Constitution. The consequence of which every *Englishman* feels to belong to him as such, and the sense he entertains of the value of those important rights and privileges which he enjoys as his birthright, endue him with a firmness and magnanimity, and inspire him with a sense of honour, and a dread of disgrace;—while his disposition, formed under the mild and genial influence of legal, orderly, and salutary Freedom, is as open, humane, and generous, as it is bold and brave. Every species of cruelty is repugnant to his nature; he is as ready to forgive and succor as to fight; and he will no more hurt or even insult a vanquished foe, than he will yield the palm of victory while he has strength to dispute it. Nor is there a People in the world so distinguished for their benevolent bounty as the *English*. Munificence and Charity are here displayed beyond all example and without ostentation; and Woe, which by the laws of Nature, is ever attendant upon the condition of Humanity, is sure among us to attract pity and relief.[17]

Liberty not only made the British the best people, but also blessed them with the best liberty, the key factor contributing to their being the best. Great Britain was the "freest nation that ever existed,"[18] enjoying "the most perfect System of Liberty ever known to mankind."[19] British "lives and liberties" were preserved "in a degree of security known to no other nation,"[20] and the kingdom was "distinguished from all others by the Liberty it enjoys."[21] The Swiss constitutionalist, J. L. De Lolme, even asserted that because of liberty "no true comparison can be made between it and the government of any other state,"[22] and the reason, according to those willing to make the most extreme claim, was that "*Britain* is the only kingdom, and *Britons* the only people who can truly say, we are free."[23]

There were two legal certainties about which everyone, Americans as well as Britons, agreed. The first was that, due to liberty, Great Britain and its constitution were "the Admiration and Envy of the World."[24] The second was that the colonies shared all the blessings of British liberty.[25] How else, asked New Jersey's John Witherspoon, could one explain the fact "that the British settlements have been improved in a proportion far beyond the settlements of other European nations." It could not be due "to the people, for they are a mixture of all nations. It must therefore be resolved singly into the degree of British liberty which they brought from home."[26]

Another difference between the concept of liberty in the eighteenth century and our ideas of liberty today was the constitutional premises on which people held liberty or the legal theories explaining the individual citizen's right to liberty. Liberty in the age of the American Revolution was not as we think of it now. It was not a series of rights withheld from government by a written constitution and protected by an independent judiciary. Nor was it a grant bestowed by government and thus, in theory, revocable by government. Liberty, rather, was an independent entity, a right in itself, separate yet interlinked with all other British rights. Liberty belonged to English and British people because they were born to it. "Inheritance" was the favorite eighteenth-century word for articulating the source or authority of the right to liberty: liberty was an inheritance like any other material, real, personal, inchoate, abstract inheritance.[27] Because the individual inherited liberty, that individual owned liberty. A central constitutional concept of eighteenth-century Great Britain was the trinity of life, liberty, and property. It is a conceptualization of human rights, "inherited" from an age before government and law were equated with power rather than right, that Thomas Jefferson altered to our everlasting loss.[28] For the constitutional trinity was not only three but one and the one was property. Life was property and liberty was property and property was protected from the whims of government not for material reasons as is sometimes suggested, but because security of property gave security to life and security to liberty. It was through the security of property that a person enjoyed true liberty: the independence that made one free. Liberty was the independence of not being beholden to any other person and—more importantly—the independence of being disdainful of government dole. It was due to the ownership of the abstract right that legal theorists in the eighteenth century thought of liberty and the security of property as one principle.[29]

In addition to property, there was another, far stronger legal foundation upon which liberty was held, liberty was defined, and liberty was protected in the eighteenth century. It was the authority of custom. When Americans during the controversy with Great Britain identified the authority for their claim to rights and, therefore, their claim to be free of arbitrary power, they usually stated that authority in the alternative. A typical instance is the Connecticut resolutions of June, 1774. The American colonists, Connecticut's assembly resolved, claimed "the rights, liberties and immunities of free-born Englishmen, to which they are justly entitled by the law of nature, by the royal grant and charter of his late Majesty King Charles the Second, and by long and uninterrupted possession."[30] It is indicative of how much our legal assumptions have changed since the eighteenth century that most students of the American Revolution would dismiss the last mentioned source of rights as not only the least important but as meaningless or not legal at all.[31] They would, instead, emphasize the claim of the authority of natural law and royal charter, the first of which, ironically, was the rhetorical window dressing of little or no significance in constitutional law,[32] and the second of which—the colonial charter— was evidence of some of the rights that Americans possessed, but by no means an authority for rights as is often supposed.[33]

In eighteenth-century legal theory and constitutional practice the strongest claim of authority for rights and liberty made by the Connecticut assembly was the assertion that the colonists were entitled to the rights of Englishmen "by long and uninterrupted possession." The legal fact proving the constitutional claim could be stated in various ways: "uninterrupted possession" (as Connecticut stated it); "uninterrupted Practice and Usage;"[34] "venerable by long Usage;"[35] "constant usage."[36] These expressions may appear to be statements of fact, but in the eighteenth century they were statements of law as well as fact: both the evidence for proving the existence of a right and the constitutional authority for that right. One may easily be misled by this appeal to the past and assume that it was an appeal to history. In truth, it was an appeal not to history but to law. Custom as constitutional authority was the opposite of history, a caricature of history. Custom was changeless time, a perspective of the past in which the civil rights or political liberty of the present existed in a timeless infinity, a frozen endless moment isolated from historical evolution, without origin, without transmission, without change, an unmeasurable duration during which there was no manifestation of sovereign will except for the implied consent of habitual acquiescence. If this misconception of historical dynamics strikes us as unsure foundations on which to rest constitutional rights, we are thinking too much as historians and not as we should—as the heirs of liberty of Sir Edward Coke. Bad law may never make good history but bad history often makes good law. The United States Supreme Court's interpretation of liberty of conscience and religion is quite often premised on unsupported history.[37] It would be unwise to doubt its validity as law.

It was, therefore, not a political boast but a statement of constitutional law to claim specific rights by saying that they had been "sanctified by long usage, a uniformity of principle and practice for ages past."[38] The constitutional principle was not only that *"long Possession* gives a Title in Law, or at least enforces it, . . . so the *publick Rights of Mankind* acquire Strength by *long Prescription,"*[39] but also (as explained by the common-law barrister who in 1777 was appointed Oxford's Vinerian professor of law) immemorial usage was "evidence of common acquiescence and consent."[40] To say that rights were known by usage was to say they were established by the conventions of civil society—conventions comprising both the practice of the rulers and the understanding of the ruled. For Americans claiming rights in the 1760s against parliamentary pretensions these conventions were proved by evidence from the English, British, and colonial past. To learn both the law ways of the rulers and the expectations of the ruled one only had to study the century and a half of colonial home rule.[41]

It was from custom, from receiving its authority from custom, that the eighteenth-century concept of liberty obtained much of its theoretical base, making it so different from the notion of liberty and the concept of civil rights in either today's Great Britain or United States. Custom ordained a constitutional world about which we read and become nostalgic, but we may wonder if it is a constitutional world in which we could ever again place our trust.

The old, customary theory of liberty was confining when compared to the theory that would emerge in both British and American constitutional law during the nineteenth century. The difference was more than the obvious reality that liberty in the eighteenth century was thought of as restraining arbitrary government rather than as liberating the individual. The offspring of a static legality that encased government in a timeless, changeless constitution, the eighteenth-century concept of liberty was torn between the constitutional ideal of freeing human subjectivity, and the constitutional reality of confining human subjectivity within the mores of a customary society. The difference was more than the theoretical gulf between a customary constitution of inherited rights and a constitution of rights reserved from an otherwise all powerful government. It was rather that the eighteenth-century expectation of government was largely the opposite of the expectations that we have in the twentieth century: the expectation of government as the decision maker; government as the provider, mover, and even the creator of liberty; government as not just the guarantor but the performer of social good. It may well be that in those contrasting expectations lies the essence of the difference between eighteenth-century constitutional theory about liberty and twentieth-century constitutional thought.[42] Lawyers have a normative designation for today's theory of legal authority. It is "positive law." Looking back we can contrast the positivistic law of now against the customary law of then in the will and pleasure of the sovereign. The eighteenth century also had words to describe the difference. They were the word "power" and the word "right." The constitutionality of an act of government or a statute or an executive order could be tested by this distinction. An act of mere power was unconstitutional. It might be legal because it could be enforced and you could be coerced into obedience, but its enforcement was itself an act of mere power. An act of right was both constitutional and legal. It was right and constitutional because it was within the accepted norms of customary law and practice, and consistent with the conventions of English or British constitutionalism.[43] "The British constitution is made to secure liberty and property," a writer told London's *Political Register* in 1770, "whatever takes away these, takes away the constitution itself, and cannot be constitutional."[44] That statement summarizes the eighteenth-century emphasis of right against power. An act of power that jeopardized established norms for securing or preserving liberty was not "constitutional." David Hartley, who was negotiator for Great Britain at the Treaty of Paris ending the American Revolution, applied the distinction when he observed that a "limited excise" (that is, one affecting only traders) "may be called a constitutional excise." A "general excise" (one permitting revenue agents to enter private houses) "is unconstitutional." The first, said Hartley, was "consistent with the liberty of the subject." The second was "totally repugnant to the freedom of our constitution."[45] The second, of course, was commanded by Parliament—a command that alone in the nineteenth century would be sufficient to make it constitutional as well as legal. In the customary world that was to crumble about Hartley with the coming of the Industrial Revolution, legislative command alone was not enough to ordain the constitutional.

The legal source and constitutional authority for liberty in the English-speaking world is but one side of the eighteenth-century liberty coin. The questions asked by the other side are what were the elements of liberty, of what did eighteenth-century liberty consist? Unfortunately for the researcher almost every political commentator in the age of the American Revolution tried his hand at defining liberty. Liberty in the eighteenth century had many definitions ranging from freedom of physical locomotion to freedom from any political restraint.[46] There was, however, a basic, core definition upon which most observers were agreed. It was that, in one form or another, liberty consisted of living under a rule of law to which the individual citizen had given consent in some form.

To understand what was meant by liberty as the rule of law, that is, the positive definition of liberty, it is necessary to ask what liberty was not—or the negative side of liberty. In the legal, political, and social theory of that day, the opposite of liberty was slavery.

We must think of slavery as the word was used in seventeenth- and eighteenth-century England, not the chattel slavery of African blacks or American Indians but the political slavery of arbitrary governmental power. That fact is graphically demonstrated by the surprising argument, often made, that political slavery, slavery that was the opposite of liberty, was a slavery that was harsher than the chattel slavery of blacks.[47]

The concept may strike us as farfetched, but in the eighteenth century chattel slavery and liberty were not incompatible. John Trenchard, writing in London, counted as one of "the Blessings of Liberty" the fact that, by purchasing British manufactures, "*English* Planters in *America*, besides maintaining themselves and ten times as many *Negroes*, maintain likewise great Numbers of their Countrymen in *England*."[48] Several decades later, during the revolutionary crisis, a South Carolinian urged his readers to support a boycott of British products by wearing "the same garb your slaves hitherto have done." They should do so, he wrote, to keep slavery out of South Carolina, a home of liberty. Liberty, the writer explained, had "found an asylum" in North America. "Learning, liberty, and every thing that ennobles the human mind, have constantly been traveling westward. I never can believe, that in this sacred land slavery shall be so soon permitted to erect her throne on the ruins of freedom."[49] It is doubtful if persons reading these words in the eighteenth century thought their author an hypocrite. There were more chattel slaves than free people in South Carolina, yet South Carolina was a land of liberty and would become a land of slavery only if Parliament made good its claim to legislature for the colonies. We will move closer to an understanding of the eighteenth-century concept of liberty if we are willing to lay aside our values and accept the notion that the existence of chattel slavery was not inconsistent with constitutional liberty even though political slavery is the opposite of constitutional liberty.

Slavery as defined in the eighteenth century was the absence of the rule of law; that is, the absence of law that protected the individual and of law limiting the power of public rulers.[50] "Only the Checks put upon Magistrates make Nations free; and only the Want of such Checks make them Slaves," John Trenchard wrote of the rule of law. "They are free, where their Magistrates are confined within certain Bounds set them by the People, and act by Rules prescribed them by the People: And they are Slaves, where their magistrates choose their own Rule, and follow their Lust and humours."[51]

There is another eighteenth-century word we have lost, that we no longer know or use as it was known or used in the eighteenth century. It is the word arbitrary, or the concept of arbitrary power. The most precise definition of slaves in the eighteenth century was people living under arbitrary rule. "In arbitrary governments," Joseph Towers point out, "all are equally slaves."[52] Everyone commenting on the matter, whether in Great Britain or her American colonies, seems to have agreed. According to eighteenth-century legal theory, there was no greater servitude than to be subject to will and pleasure. "[A] vague and indefinite obedience, to the fluctuating and arbitrary will of any superior, is the most abject and complete slavery."[53]

There was no concept more dynamic, more exegetic, or more useful for eighteenth-century politics and law than the concept of arbitrary power. The notion of arbitrariness appears in the polemic literature as frequently as any other concept except liberty, slavery, and constitution. For both constitutional law and nonconstitutional public law it was the most hermeneutic concept, serving more than any other to define law and set theoretical limits to governmental actions. There was no accusation against an official more serious than that he sought to impose arbitrary rule. It had been the first count in the act of attainder against the earl of Strafford, an article in the impeachment of the judges who rendered the shipmoney decision, one of the major charges justifying the execution of Charles I, and part of the indictment against George III in the American Declaration of Independence.[54]

Arbitrary power should not be thought of as abuse of authority. Nor should it be associated with any form of government, as it can exist under a democracy as much as under a monarchy, aristocracy, or oligarchy. Rather, tyrannical power is abuse of power, arbitrary power is power without restraint.[55] "[N]o liberty can subsist where there is such power," Sydney wrote in the seventeenth century,[56] and his words were echoed on both sides of the ocean in the age of the American Revolution when the contrast was between arbitrariness and liberty. "The idea of an unlimited power is inconsistent with the genius of liberty," a South Carolinian observed.[57] "For liberty cannot exist where oppression may be exercised without controul," a London pamphleteer explained.[58] "[I]n a state where discretion begins, law, liberty, and safety end," King George III was warned.[59]

The warning to the king was in a petition from the freeholders of Middlesex, generally regarded as the most radical element on the British political scene. But what they said to George III was hardly radical by eighteenth-century constitutional norms. It was that under arbitrary government there could be neither liberty nor law, for arbitrary power, like slavery, was not only the opposite or the "end" of liberty, it was also the opposite of law, and in that fact lies the most important element in the positive definition of liberty.

Just as people thought the "rule of law" the opposite of arbitrary power[60]— "Law and arbitrary power are at eternal hostility," Edmund Burke asserted[61]— so they thought of law as the central pillar of liberty. That law—the law that the friends of liberty trusted to protect liberty—was not a code of substantive rules or guiding principles. Nor was it the command of the sovereign. It was, rather, restraint on arbitrary power—the old law, the folk law, the good law, the customary law of the community.[62] Today we know that even in 1776 this notion of law was already superannuated. Most legal theorists then were not aware of the change and still thought of law as sovereign, not as the manifestation of sovereignty. As a result, when they described law as the foundation of liberty, they meant the old law that was not the sovereign's command but the sovereign's restraint.[63]

This law that restrained the sovereign was sometimes said to emanate from the people to limit magistrates. The contention deserves scrutiny as it may be easily misread. Eighteenth-century legal or political theorists who would have had magistrates subject to "the people" did not want the law that protected liberty to emanate from those people in the form of the arbitrary and capricious will of the majority. The law that was liberty's foundation checked the ruling majority as well as the aristocratic magistracy or the hereditary monarchy. "The primary aim, therefore, of all well-framed Constitutions," an American loyalist wrote in words acceptable to whigs as well as to tories, "is, to place man, as it were, out of the reach of his own power, and also out of the power of others as weak as himself, by placing him under the power of law."[64]

Just what the bounds were confining magistrates was a topic seldom discussed in the eighteenth century. Generalities, not particularities, provided the norms of eighteenth-century jurisprudence. Specific guarantees of individual rights characterizing twentieth-century legal theory seldom were mentioned in the age of the American Revolution. Rights recognized by law or expounded in theory were constitutional rights and termed natural primarily for embellishment. Indeed, eighteenth-century thought about liberty was so attuned to the existing constitution and so removed from the ideal that many rights recognized today were thought of then in opposite ways. Religious tolerance is an example. It was not just a matter that the concept of liberty did not require that Catholics be treated equally to Protestants. Rather, principles were so dependent on the current constitution that a proposal to allow Catholics to be candidates for public office in one of the ceded islands could be condemned as contrary to liberty. The possibility that Catholics might stand in elections was said to be an "outrageous violation of the laws of England, of the constitution of this colony, and of the liberty of the subject."[65]

Due to the emphasis upon generalities rather than specifics most eighteenth-century discussion of the law of liberty dealt with sweeping principles rather than with individual privileges. Perhaps the closest that eighteenth-century writers came to stating particularities was when the end of law was considered in terms that today might seem too broad to be a guide for governmental conduct. One example is Blackstone's maxim that the "first and primary end of human laws is to maintain and regulate these absolute rights of individuals."[66] Another was Locke's frequently quoted principle that the *end of law* is not to abolish or restrain, but *to preserve and enlarge Freedom.*[67] In terms of constitutional theory, the principle could be stated as a limitation on government action with liberty defining the limits. In Great Britain in 1776, Henry Goodricke argued that "the end of Government is only to restrain an injurious exercise of private liberty, that is, licentiousness."[68] In Massachusetts that same year, Samuel West told the General Court that "the end and design of civil government, cannot be to deprive men of their liberty, or take away their freedom; but on the contrary the true design of civil government is to protect men in the enjoyment of liberty."[69]

We would misinterpret the eighteenth-century legal mind were we to suppose that people at that time thought these sweeping maxims meaningless platitudes. William Blackstone believed he was stating a practical, substantive theorem when he claimed that "civil liberty is the natural liberty of mankind, so far restrained by human laws as is necessary for the good of society."[70] This test—whether stated as "the good of society" or "the enjoyment of liberty"— was the most particular and precise criterion stated in the eighteenth century for setting the limits of liberty. Applying that criterion, civil liberty was said to exist when a person was free "from all restraints except such as established law imposes, for the good of the community,"[71] or, as Blackstone observed in his *Commentaries*, "that system of laws, is alone calculated to maintain civil liberty, which leaves the subject entire master of his own conduct, except in those points wherein the public good requires some direction or restraint."[72]

Blackstone's theorem is a measure of how far we in the twentieth century have departed from the liberty that was the lodestar of our founding ancestors. If liberty was to be secure, Blackstone said, law should be for the good of society. But how was the good of society determined? One of today's prevailing theories would have it determined by the administrative effectiveness of a particular rule or the benefit government could direct on the community by promulgating a particular rule. That would not have been the eighteenth century's answer. A criterion of the law's "goodness" in the eighteenth century— not the only criterion, perhaps, but surely the dominant one—was the degree to which it freed the individual from government direction. Put another way, the less a law restrained the citizen, and the more it restrained government, the better the law. Stated positively, the rule was that the "[s]ociety whose laws least restrain the words and actions of its members, is most free."[73] Stated negatively, it was that "every causeless or unnecessary restraint of the Will is an infringement of that political freedom to which every member of society is entitled."[74] The "goodness" of law was at its most acceptable best when the noninterventionist state avoided the type of "law" that is legislative promulgation because it, the government or the legislature, was restrained by the type of "law" promulgated by customary legal or constitutional norms.

It is worth giving close—very close—attention to the notion that law is restraint on government rather than restraint on people and then asking whether eighteenth-century liberty was founded on values we no longer comprehend and which no longer command our allegiance. The question asked in the introduction of this essay, whether we and the founding fathers share the same idea of liberty or share only a drastically transmuted word, may depend for an answer not on whether it is possible to determine the "original intent" concerning liberty, but whether we are able to appreciate how little relevance the "original understanding" of the framers holds for the dominant American school of legal and constitutional theory in the last two decades of the twentieth century. What is the jurisprudential value of the "original understanding" for a constitutional philosophy that has abandoned the liberty of restrained government for the liberty of expectations fulfilled by government largess? One small, but striking, measure of how much we have lost the concept of liberty-as-restraint is the number of law professors teaching in accredited law schools who confuse as "law" some of the arguments of the critical-legal-studies movement. Consider a recent attack on the principle of the rule of law: not the rule of law known to the founders, but our anemic, attenuated rule of law as it barely exists today.

> Unless we are prepared to succumb to Hobbesian pessimism . . . I do not see how a Man of the Left can describe the rule of law as "an unqualified human good." It undoubtedly restrains power, but it also prevents power's benevolent exercise. It creates formal equality—a not inconsiderable virtue—but it *promotes* substantive inequality by creating a consciousness that radically separates law from politics, means from ends, processes from outcomes. By promoting procedural justice it enables the shrewd, the calculating, and the wealthy to manipulate its forms to their own advantage. And it ratifies and legitimates an adversarial, competitive, and atomistic conception of human relations.[75]

It is indicative of how much the perception of liberty has changed in two hundred years that what may be passed off as an argument for liberty in the twentieth century is indisputably a resurrection of eighteenth-century "slavery." It is worth recalling that it was not just mainstream constitutional thinkers, but also "radicals" who in the eighteenth century warned that "in a state where discretion begins, law, liberty, and safety end"[76]—a law, a liberty, and a safety we no longer know or care about. Of course, this vision of a constitutionalism without the rule of law will never be taken seriously by the majority of American lawyers, but the very fact that it can be suggested provides a warning of how difficult it is to compare the eighteenth-century radical fear of "discretion" to the concept of liberty promulgated by those members of today's judiciary who decree that the executive and legislative branches must promote the interventionist state. So much have some familiar words of the American legal vocabulary been altered that, even for those who retain some respect for the rule of law, the basic eighteenth-century common-law dichotomy between power and right no longer is understood to be a rule of law, as "right" is now compounded with social good and "power" is justified by the mere promulgation of that new legal "right."[77]

It was arbitrary power that the eighteenth century feared would be the death of liberty. It is to arbitrary power that we have succumbed. Perhaps all we have left is to lament, yet the principle of the rule of law is still the opposite of arbitrary power and it may be that, despite today's judicial instrumentalism,[78] the theory, although not the reality, survives.[79] Somewhere beneath the rubble of the original structure there remains some vitality to the admonition that ours was to be a government of laws and not of men. Although we have become a government in which the human factor has been restored by redefining "law" to include judicial discretion, we should not surrender all hope that somehow we can regain some semblance of what the founders of the republic meant by liberty and even of the original understanding about the meaning and the role of law.

New York University School of Law

NOTES

*The research for this study was supported by the Filomen D'Agostino Greenberg and Max E. Greenberg Faculty Research Fund of New York University School of Law. The eighteenth-century material outlined in this article is more extensively elaborated in *The Concept of Liberty in the Age of the American Revolution* (Chicago, 1988).

1. "[T]he ascendency of what has been called the new social history, which focuses on the activities of the humbler segments of society rather than 'great white men,' practically proscribed the Constitution as a topic of investigation. As a result, many professional historians believe that they have 'no stake in the Constitution,' a remark that passed without reproof from the members of the fraternity assembled at a recent conference. The passing of history from college curriculums because of its perceived irrelevance, documented by recent surveys, is surely related to the pervasiveness of such attitudes in the academy," James H. Hutson, "James Madison, Minus Halo," *New York Times Book Review*, 2 March 1986, p. 19, col. 1.

2.

> Over the last decade, people who write about constitutional law have been debating a question so abstract that those who focus on it have come to call themselves theorists. The question is whether the constitutional text should be the sole source of law for the purposes of judicial review, or whether judges should supplement the text with an unwritten constitution that is implicit in precedent, practice, and conventional morality. Abstract as the question is, it implicates important issues of how much power judges should have in government.

Thomas C. Grey, "The Constitution as Scripture," *Stanford Law Review*, 37 (1984): 1. For entries in the debate, see Michael Perry, "The Authority of Text, Tradition, and Reason: A Theory of Constitutional Interpretation," *Southern California Law Review*, 58 (1985): 551; H. Jefferson Powell, "The Original Understanding of Original Intent," *Harvard Law Review*, 98 (1985): 885; David A. J. Richards, "Interpretation and Historiography," *Southern California Law Review*, 58 (1985): 489; Harry Wellington, "History and Morals in Constitutional Adjudication," *Harvard Law Review*, 97 (1983): 326;

David A. J. Richards, "The Aims of Constitutional Theory," *University of Dayton Law Review*, 8 (1983): 723; Earl Maltz, "Some New Thoughts on an Old Problem—The Role of the Intent of the Framers in Constitutional Theory," *Boston University Law Review*, 63 (1983): 811; Owen Fiss, "Objectivity and Interpretation," *Stanford Law Review*, 34 (1982): 739; Frederick Schauer, "An Essay on Constitutional Language," *U.C.L.A. Law Review*, 29 (1982): 797; Jeff Powell, "The Compleat Jeffersonian: Justice Rehnquist and Federalism," *Yale Law Journal*, 91 (1982): 1317; Paul Brest, "Interpretation and Interest," *Stanford Law Review*, 34 (1982): 765; Ronald Dworkin, "The Forum of Principle," *New York University Law Review*, 56 (1981): 469. See also for a specific argument concerning the Eleventh Amendment, Gary J. Simson, "The Role of History in Constitutional Interpretation: A Case Study," *Cornell Law Review*, 70 (1985): 253.

3. As it has been for those judges given to writing historical nonsense. See e.g., *post* note 37.

4. "Liberty" has been used sparingly as a normative concept in this century. One instance is Brandeis, J.: "Despite arguments to the contrary which had seemed to me persuasive, it is settled that the due process clause of the Fourteenth Amendment applies to matters of substantive law as well as matters of procedure. Thus all fundamental rights comprised within the term liberty are protected by the Federal Constitution from invasion by the States." Whitney v. California, 274 U.S. 357, 373 (1926) (concurring opinion).

5. Richard Price, *Observations on the Nature and Value of Civil Liberty, the Principles of Government, and the Justice and Policy of this War with America* [eighth edition, 1778], reprinted in Richard Price, *Two Tracts on Civil Liberty, the War with America, and the Debts and Finances of the Kingdom: with a General Introduction and Supplement* (London, 1778), 5.

6. Anonymous, *Experience Preferable to Theory. An Answer to Dr. Price's Observations on the Nature of Civil Liberty, and the Justice and Policy of the War with America* (London, 1776), 17.

7. The topic of the rhetoric of liberty in the eighteenth century has been either overlooked or ignored. For a brief recognition of its importance in the colonies, see Alice M. Baldwin, *The New England Clergy and the American Revolution* (New York, 1928), 88-89 (hereafter cited as Baldwin).

8. Brutus, "To the Inhabitants of Virginia," 19 May 1775, *American Archives: Fourth Series. Containing a Documentary History of the English Colonies in North America from the King's Message to Parliament, of March 7, 1774, to the Declaration of Independence of the United States*, 2 (Washington, D.C. 1839): 641 (hereafter cited as 2 *American Archives*).

9. Letter from AEquus, 16 January 1766, *London Magazine*, 35 (1766): 34.

10. Anonymous, *Justice and Policy. An Essay on the Increasing Growth and Enormities of our Great Cities* (Dublin, 1772), 16.

11. Anonymous, *Serious and Impartial Observations on the Blessings of Liberty and Peace Addressed to Persons of all Parties. Inviting them also to enter into that Grand ASSOCIATION, which is able to secure the Safety and Happiness of the British Empire* (London, 1776), 6.

12. Anonymous, *A Fair Trial of the Important Question, or the Rights of Election As-serted; Against the Doctrine of Incapacity by Expulsion, or by Resolution: Upon True Constitutional Principles, the Real Law of Parliament, the Common Right of the Sub-ject, and the Determinations of the House of Commons* (London, 1769), 234 footnote.

13. Anonymous, *What Should be Done: or, Remarks on the Political State of Things. Addressed to the Present Administration, the Members of the House of Commons, and the Good People of England* (London, 1766), 34.

14. [Hugh Hume, Earl of Marchmont,] *A Serious Exhortation to the Electors of Great Britain: Wherein the Importance of the approaching Elections is particularly proved from our present Situation both at Home and Abroad* (London, 1740), 39.

15. Anonymous, *A Critical Review of the Liberties of British Subjects. With a Compar-ative View of the Proceedings of the H[ous]e of C[ommon]s of I[relan]d, against an unfortunate Exile of that Country; who, in contending for the Rights and Liberties of the Publick, lost his own* (second edition, London, 1750), 11 (quoting Charles Lucas).

16. From liberty, a typical claim asserted, "has arisen the prosperity, the wealth, the splendour of GREAT BRITAIN. It is Liberty that has given cultivation to our fields, that has enlarged our cities, that has extended our commerce, and that has enabled us to make those advances in science and literature, which have given celebrity to our coun-try throughout every quarter of the world." Joseph Towers, *An Oration Delivered at the London Tavern, on the Fourth of November, 1788, on the Occasion of the Com-memoration of the Revolution, and the Completion of a Century from that Great Event* (London, 1788), 30.

17. [John Bowles,] *Dialogues on the Rights of Britons, between a Farmer, a Sailor, and a Manufacturer. Dialogue the Second* (London, second edition, 1792), 20-21.

18. Anonymous, *British Liberties, or the Free-born Subject's Inheritance; Containing the Laws that form the Basis of those Liberties, with Observations thereon; also an Introductory Essay on Political Liberty and a Comprehensive View of the Constitution of Great Britain* (London, 1766), vii.

19. [George Rous,] *The Claim of the House of Commons, to a Negative on the Ap-pointment of Ministers by the Crown, Examined and Confuted* (London, 1784), 4.

20. Anonymous, *A Dialogue on the Actual State of Parliament* (Dublin, 1783), 33.

21. Anonymous, *A Candid Examination of the Legality of the Warrant Issued by the Secretaries of State for Apprehending the Printers, Publishers, &c. of a late Interesting Paper* (London, 1764), 3.

22. J. L. De Lolme, *The Constitution of England; or, an Account of the English Govern-ment; in which it is Compared Both with the Republican Form of Government, and the Other Monarchies in Europe* (new edition, London, 1807), 490-491.

23. H. T. Dickinson, *Liberty and Property: Political Ideology in Eighteenth-Century Britain* (New York, 1977), 143 (quoting *An Essay on Liberty and Independency* [1747]). See also Instructions of Deputies from Pennsylvania Counties to Representatives, 21 July 1774, *London Magazine*, 43 (1774): 585; Algernon Sydney, *Discourses Concerning Government*, reprinted in *The Works of Algernon Sydney: A New Edition* (London, 1772), 499 (hereafter cited as Sydney, *Discourses*); [Arthur Young,] *Political Essays Concerning the Present State of the British Empire* (London, 1772), 21.

24. Thomas Barnard, *A Sermon Preached before His Excellency Francis Bernard, Esq.; Governor and Commander in Chief, the Honourable His Majesty's Council, and the Honourable House of Representatives, of the Province of the Massachusetts-Bay in New England, May 25th, 1763. Being the Anniversary for the Election of His Majesty's Council for said Province* (Boston, 1763), 37; Anonymous, *The Court of Star Chamber, or Seat of Oppression* (London, 1768), 16; William Allen, *The American Crisis: A Letter, Addressed by Permission to the Earl Gower, Lord President of the Council, &c. &c. &c. On the present alarming Disturbances in the Colonies* (London, 1774), 48. Similarly see John Wright, *The Speech of John Wright, Esq; One of the Magistrates of Lancaster County, to the Court and Grand-Jury, on his Removal from the Commission of the Peace at the Quarter-Sessions held at Lancaster for the said County in May 1741* [Philadelphia, 1741], 2; Anonymous, *A Letter on Parliamentary Representation, in which the Propriety of Triennial and Septennial Parliaments is Considered. Inscribed to John Sinclair, Esq. M.P.* (London, second edition, 1783), 28.

25. Baldwin, *supra* note 7, p. 86 (quoting Nathaniel Hunn); Nathaniel Hunn, *The Welfare of a Government Considered. A Sermon Preach'd before the General Assembly of the Colony of Connecticut, at Hartford, on the Day of their Anniversary Election, May 14th, 1747* (New London, 1747), 17-18, 24; Stephen White, *Civil Rulers Gods by Office, and the Duties of such Considered and Enforced. A Sermon Preached before the General Assembly of the Colony of Connecticut, at Hartford, on the Day of their Anniversary Election, May the 12th, 1763* (New London, 1763), 23; William Welsteed, *The Dignity and Duty of the Civil Magistrate. A Sermon Preached in the Audience of His Honour, Spencer Phips, Esq; Lieutenant Governour and Commander in Chief, the Honourable His Majesty's Council, and the Honourable House of Representatives, of the Province of the Massachusetts-Bay, in New-England, May 29th 1751. Being the Anniversary for the Election of His Majesty's Council for the said Province* (Boston, 1751), 33; Address of Judge William Henry Drayton to the Camden District (S.C.) Grand Jury, November Session, 1774, *London Magazine*, 44 (1775): 126.

26. Clinton Rossiter, *The Seedtime of the Republic: The Origin of the American Tradition of Political Life* (New York, 1953), 349 (quoting Witherspoon).

27. Contrary to some recent scholarship, the eighteenth-, indeed the seventeenth-century concept of property covered the abstract as well as the physical and in the nineteenth century the definition of property did not change to the extent that critics of the "rule of law" wish to claim. See e.g. Kenneth J. Vandevelde, "The New Property of the Nineteenth Century: The Development of the Modern Concept of Property," *Buffalo Law Review*, 29 (1980): 330-333, 366-367.

28. It has recently been asserted that "Jeffersonians thought rights inalienable precisely because they had roots inherent in the human being. That property right was not similarly viewed by Jefferson to have such inherent roots is also clear from his substitution of 'pursuit of happiness' for Locke's 'property'." David M. Post, "Jeffersonian Revisions of Locke: Education, Property-Rights, and Liberty," *Journal of the History of Ideas*, 47 (1986): 147, 152. Possibly, but it should also be kept in mind that Jefferson with his "inherent" hostility to the common law and British constitutionalism—a legal tradition that "habituated" the "living generation" to custom and made the individual free of the arbitrariness of the living majority—knew that he was repudiating one of the sources of constitutional government. It has also been said that, "For Jeffersonians human nature

indicated a basic set of rights, but property was incidental and adventitious, a right produced only after formation of a social contract, a social rather than a natural right," ibid. The idea that the right to property in the eighteenth century was a "natural" right in the meaning here, is primarily the invention of twentieth-century historians. The belief here attributed to Jefferson was held by all common lawyers, even Blackstone who is often misrepresented. What separated Jefferson from the common-law tradition was not the definition of the right to property, but the concept of the security of property. For Blackstone, see Robert P. Burns, "Blackstone's Theory of the 'Absolute' Rights of Property," *Cincinnati Law Review*, 54 (1985): 67-86. For the "positivism" of property in the eighteenth century, see William Michael Treanor, "The Origins and Original Significance of the Just Compensation Clause of the Fifth Amendment," *Yale Law Journal*, 94 (1985): 694-716.

29. Thus, the "preferred Freedoms" distinction between "political" rights and "economic" rights drawn by the Supreme Court not only would have had no appeal for eighteenth-century Americans, it is likely they might have thought it "anti-liberty." United States v. Carolene Products Co., 304 U.S. 144, 152n4 (1938) (per Stone, J.).

30. Connecticut Resolutions, June 1774, *Revolutionary Virginia The Road to Independence—Volume II: The Committees and the Second Convention, 1773-1775. A Documentary Record*, compiled by William J. Van Schreeven and Robert L. Scribner (Charlottesville, Virginia, 1975): 116. "[T]he inhabitants of the *English* Colonies of *North America*, [had rights] by the immutable laws of nature, the principles of the *English* Constitution, and the several Charters or compacts," Resolves of Georgia Commons House of Assembly, January 1775, *American Archives: Fourth Series. Containing a Documentary History of the English Colonies in North America from the King's Message to Parliament, of March 7, 1774, to the Declaration of Independence by the United States* 1 (Washington, 1837): 1156 (hereafter cited as *American Archives*). For discussion, see John Phillip Reid, *Constitutional History of the American Revolution: The Authority of Rights* (Madison, Wisconsin, 1986), 81-168.

31. Jack P. Greene, "From the Perspective of Law: Context and Legitimacy in the Origins of the American Revolution," *South Atlantic Quarterly*, 85 (1986): 56-57, 69-73.

32. John Phillip Reid, "The Irrelevance of the Declaration," in *Law in the American Revolution and the Revolution in the Law—A Collection of Review Essays on American Legal History*, edited by Hendrik Hartog (New York, 1981), 47-69.

33. In the eighteenth century constitutional possession constituted a stronger constitutional claim than did charter. For the irrelevance of charter, see "Monitor V" [Arthur Lee], *Virginia Gazette* (Rind), 24 March 1768, p. 1, col. 1; Reid, "In the First Line of Defense: The Colonial Charters, the Stamp Act Debate and the Coming of the American Revolution," *New York University Law Review*, 51 (1976): 177-215.

34. New York Petition to King George III, 18 October 1764, *Journal of the Votes and Proceedings of the General Assembly of the Colony of New-York. Began the 8th Day of November, 1743; and Ended the 23d of December, 1765. Vol. II. Published by Order of the General Assembly* (New York, 1766), 770.

35. Instructions of Providence, 13 August 1765, *Boston Evening-Post*, 19 August 1765, p. 2, col. 2.

36. Resolves of Virginia's Richmond County (29 June 1774) and Caroline County (14 July 1774), *American Archives, supra* note 30, pp. 492, 540.

37. Brandeis, J., contended without any documentation except for a reference to Jefferson:

> Those who won our independence believed that the final end of the State was to make men free to develop their faculties; and that in its government the deliberative forces should prevail over the arbitrary. They valued liberty both as an end and as a means. They believed liberty to be the secret of happiness and courage to be the secret of liberty.

Whitney v. California, 274 U.S. 357, 375 (1926) (concurring opinion).

38. [Joseph Hawley,] "To the Inhabitants. . . ," 13 April 1775, *American Archives, supra* note 8, p. 332.

39. *Craftsman*, (No. 466, 7 June 1735) 14: 2.

40. Richard Wooddeson, *Elements of Jurisprudence Treated of in the Preliminary Part of a Course of Lectures on the Law of England* (Dublin, 1792), 35. For a leading English appeal to custom for authority of rights, see Petition of Grievances (1610), *State Trials*, 2: 519-520. For an American lay understanding, see Charles Chauncy, *A Discourse on "the good News from a far Country." Deliver'd July 24th. A Day of Thanks-giving to Almighty God, throughout the Province of the Massachusetts-Bay in New-England, on Occasion of the Repeal of the STAMP-ACT* (Boston, 1766), 15 (hereafter cited as Chauncy, *Discourse*). For an early explanation by a royalist judge, see David Jenkins, *Lex Terrae; or, Laws of the Land* (1647), reprinted in *A Collection of Scarce and Valuable Tracts, on the Most Interesting and Entertaining Subjects: But Chiefly such as Relate to the History and Constitution of these Kingdoms. Selected from an Infinite Number in Print and Manuscript, in the Royal, Cotton, Sion, and Other Public, as well as Private, Libraries; Particularly that of the Late Lord Somers*, edited by Walter Scott, 5 (London, 1815): 98-114.

41. "That it is the just right and privilege of his Majesty's liege subjects of this Colony to be governed by their General Assembly in the article of taxing, and internal police, agreeable to the powers and privileges recognised and confirmed in the Royal Charters aforesaid, which they have enjoyed for more than a century past, and have neither forfeited nor surrendered, but the same have been constantly recognised by the King and Parliament of *Great Britain*," Resolutions of the Connecticut House of Representatives, May 1774, *American Archives, supra* note 30, p. 356. For similar examples from the colonial past, see Speech of the Speaker to the Lieutenant Governor, 11 November 1736, *South-Carolina Gazette*, 20 November 1736, p. 2, col. 1; A. E. Dick Howard, *The Road from Runnymede: Magna Carta and Constitutionalism in America* (Charlottesville, Virginia, 1968), 29, 51. See also [George Channing,] *A Letter to the Right Honourable Wills Earl of Hillsborough, on the Connection between Great Britain and her American Colonies* (London, 1768), 17; Chauncy, *Discourse, supra* note 40, p. 14.

42. It must be appreciated that this was not understood in the eighteenth century to be a constitutional defense of the political or economic status quo, but a necessary ingredient for the defense of liberty. People in the age of the American Revolution would not have accepted the choice postulated by the extreme of today's legal scholarship—they would not have believed it.

The defense of the received forms of doctrine has always rested on an implicit
challenge: either accept the ruling style, with its aggressive contrast to controversy
over the basic terms of social life, as the true form of doctrine, or find yourself
reduced to the inconclusive contest of political visions. This dilemma is merely one
of the many specific conceptual counterparts to the general choice: either re-
sign yourself to some established version of social order, or face the war of all
against all.

Roberto Mangabeira Unger, "The Critical Legal Studies Movement," *Harvard Law Review*, 96 (1983): 576-577.

43. Reid, "In the Taught Tradition: The Meaning of Law in Massachusetts-Bay Two
Hundred Years Ago," *Suffolk University Law Review*, 14 (1980): 931-974 (hereafter
cited as "Taught Tradition").

44. *Political Register*, 7 (1770): 152.

45. [David Hartley,] *The Right of Appeal to Juries, in Causes of Excise, Asserted* (London, [1763]), 4.

46. This definition was less often stated than it was implied by those wishing to dispar-
age it. Thus the archbishop of York complained: "I have sometimes thought it a misfor-
tune, that a thing so valuable and important, should have no word in our language to
express it, except one which goes to every thing that is wild and lawless," William
Markham, *A Sermon Preached before the Incorporated Society for the Propagation of
the Gospel in Foreign Parts, at their Anniversary Meeting, in the Parish Church of St.
Mary-le-Bow, on Friday, February 21, 1777* (London, 1777), 19.

47. Baron de Montesquieu, *The Spirit of Laws. Translated from the French of M. de
Secondat, Baron de Montesquieu, by Mr. Nugent*, vol. 1 (second edition, London,
1752): 336 (hereafter cited as Montesquieu); Anonymous, *The Evidence of the Com-
mon and Statute Laws of the Realm; Usage, Records, History with the Greatest and
Best Authorities Down to the 3d of George the IIId, in Proof of the Rights of Britons
Throughout the British Empire. Addressed to the People* (London, 1775), 13-14;
[Edward Long,] *Candid Reflections Upon the Judgement lately awarded by the Court of
King's Bench in Westminster-Hall, On What is commonly called the Negroe-Cause, by
a Planter* (London, 1772), 73-74.

48. Letter of 24 February 1721, *Cato's Letters: or, Essays on Liberty, Civil and Religious, And other Important Subjects. In Four Volumes*, vol. 2 (sixth edition, London,
1755): 310.

49. "To the Inhabitants of . . . South Carolina," *American Archives, supra* note 30,
p. 512.

50. One form of arbitrary power was government free of the rule of law. "Power unlimited," according to a colonial newspaper, "would be absolute Slavery," *Boston Gazette*, 10 May 1756, p. 1, col. 1. Montesquieu labeled as "slaves" the subjects of despotic
governments in which rule was not by law but by will and caprice, Montesquieu, *supra*
note 47, p. 37. See also, Instructions to Representatives in Parliament, 24 June 1773,
*Addresses, Remonstrances, and Petitions; Commencing the 24th of June, 1769, Pre-
sented to the King and Parliament, from the Court of Common Council, and the Livery
in Common Hall assembled, with his Majesty's Answers: Likewise the Speech to the*

King, made by the late Mr. Alderman Beckford, When Lord Mayor of the City of London (London, [1778]), 40-43; Francis Dobbs, *A Letter to the Right Honourable Lord North, on his Propositions in Favour of Ireland* (Dublin, 1780), 10; J. J. Zubly, "To Lord Dartmouth," *London Magazine*, 45 (1776): 38; Sydney, *Discourses, supra* note 23, p. 10; [Stephen Johnson,] *Some Important Observations, Occasioned by, and adapted to, The Publick Fast, Ordered by Authority, December 18th, A.D. 1765. On Account of the peculiar Circumstances of the Present Day* (Newport, R.I., 1766), 34 (hereafter cited as [Johnson,] *Observations*).

51. Trenchard, Letter of 9 February 1722, *Cato's Letters, supra* note 48, vol. 4, p. 81; Caleb Evans, *British Constitutional Liberty. A Sermon Preached at Broad-mead, Bristol, November 5, 1775* (Bristol, [1775]), 27. See also Anonymous, *The Political Balance in which the Principles and Conduct of the Two Parties are weighed* (London, 1765), 16; [William Stevens,] *The Revolution Vindicated, and Constitutional Liberty Asserted. In Answer to the Reverend Dr. Watson's Accession Sermon, Preached before the University of Cambridge, on October 25th, 1776* (Cambridge, 1777), 51; Peter Peckard, *The Nature and Extent of Civil and Religious Liberty. A Sermon Preached before the University of Cambridge, November the 5th, 1783* (Cambridge, 1783), 8.

52. [Joseph Towers,] *A Letter to the Rev. Mr. John Wesley; In Answer to his late Pamphlet, Entitled, "Free Thoughts on the Present State of Public Affairs"* (London, 1771), 11.

53. Anonymous, *Reflections on Government, With Respect to America. To Which is Added, Carmen Latinum* (London, 1766), 14. See also [John Wilkes,] *A Letter to Samuel Johnson, L.L.D.* ([London,] 1770), 42-43; [Johnson,] *Observations, supra* note 50, p. 7; Jared Eliot, *Give Cesar his Due. Or, the Obligation that Subjects are under to their Civil Rulers, As was shewed in a Sermon Preach'd before the General Assembly of the Colony of Connecticut at Hartford, May the 11th, 1738. The Day for the Election of the Honourable the Governour, the Deputy-Governour, and the Worshipful Assistants* (New London, Connecticut, 1738), 36 footnote; "To the Worthy Inhabitants of . . . Boston," 21 July 1774, *American Archives, supra* note 30, p. 627.

54. Reid, "In Legitimate Stirps: The Concept of 'Arbitrary,' the Supremacy of Parliament, and the Coming of the American Revolution," *Hofstra Law Review*, 5 (1977): 459-499.

55. Abraham D. Kriegel, "Liberty and Whiggery in Early Nineteenth-century England," *Journal of Modern History*, 52 (1980): 260.

56. Sydney, *Discourses, supra* note 23, p. 386.

57. *South-Carolina Gazette*, 18 January 1768, p. 1, col. 4.

58. Anonymous, *Resistance no Rebellion: In Answer to Doctor Johnson's Taxation no Tyranny* (London, 1775), 17.

59. Petition of Middlesex to the King, June 1769, *The Cambridge Magazine: or Universal Repository of Arts, Sciences, and the Belle Letters. For the Year MDCCLXIX* (London, 1769), 219.

60. E. P. Thompson, *Whigs and Hunters: The Origin of the Black Act* (New York, 1975), 265-266 (hereafter cited as Thompson, *Hunters*).

61. James Louis Montrose, *Precedent in English Law and Other Essays*, edited by

Harold Grenville Hanbury (Shannon, Ireland, 1968), 42 (quoting Edmund Burke).

62. "Taught Tradition," *supra* note 43, pp. 931-974; Reid, *In Defiance of the Law: The Standing-Army Controversy, the Two Constitutions, and the Coming of the American Revolution* (Chapel Hill, N.C., 1981), 32-49.

63. Anonymous, *The True Merits of a Late Treatise, printed in America, Intitled, Common Sense, Addressed to the Inhabitants of America. By a late Member of the Continental Congress, a Native of a Republican State* (London, 1776), iii; Trenchard, Letter of 9 February 1722, *Cato's Letters, supra* note 48, vol. 4, p. 81.

64. Jonathan Boucher, *A View of the Causes and Consequences of the American Revolution; in Thirteen Discourses, Preached in North America between the Years 1763 and 1775; With an Historical Preface* (London, 1797), 363. See also Montesquieu, *supra* note 47, pp. 262-263; John Locke, *Two Treatises of Government: A Critical Edition with an Introduction and Apparatus Criticus,* edited by Peter Laslett (second edition, Cambridge, 1967), Book 2, Sec. 57 (hereafter cited as Locke, *Two Treatises*); A. J. Carlyle, *Political Liberty: A History of the Conception in the Middle Ages and Modern Times* (Oxford, 1941), 148.

65. Letter from Arthur Piggot to "the Gentlemen Electors of the Town of St. George, Grenada," 21 January 1772, *Political Register,* 10 (1772): 293. See also George Rudé, "The London 'Mob' of the Eighteenth Century," *Historical Journal,* 2 (1959): 14-15.

66. Ernest Barker, *Essays on Government* (Oxford, 1945), 140 (quoting Blackstone).

67. James Tully, *A Discourse on Property: John Locke and His Adversaries* (Cambridge, 1980), 44 (quoting Locke); John Forster, *Two Sermons Preached at Northampton Assizes, April 7 and July 20, 1757* (Cambridge, 1757), 37 (quoting Locke); Peter Laslett, Introduction to Locke, *Two Treatises, supra* note 64, p. 111.

68. [Henry Goodricke,] *Observations on Dr. Price's Theory and Principles of Civil Liberty and Government, Preceded by a Letter to a Friend on the Pretensions of the American Colonies, in Respect of Right and Equity* (York, 1776), 87-88.

69. Samuel West, *A Sermon Preached Before the Honorable Council, and the Honorable House of Representatives, of the Colony of the Massachusetts-Bay, in New-England. May 29th, 1776. Being the Anniversary for the Election of the Honorable Council for the Colony* (Boston, 1776), 14.

70. William Blackstone, *Tracts Chiefly Relating to the Antiquities and Laws of England* (third edition, Oxford, 1771), 19.

71. William Markham, "Sermon Preached," reprinted in Bernard Peach, *Richard Price and the Ethical Foundations of the American Revolution* (Durham, N.C., 1979), 263; Mystagogus Candidus, *Two Letters: viz. I. A Letter to the Earl of Abingdon, in which his Grace of York's Notions of Civil Liberty are Examined by Liberalis; Published in the London Evening Post, November 6th, 1777. II. Vera Icon; or a Vindication of his Grace of York's Sermon, preached on February 21st, 1777* (London, 1777), 4.

72. William Blackstone, *Commentaries on the Laws of England,* 1 (Oxford, 1765): 122.

73. Clinton Rossiter, *The Political Thought of the American Revolution* (New York, 1963), 122 (quoting the *Boston Gazette,* 1767). This maxim should not be confused with ideas associated with Jeffersonianism. Jeffersonianism would have destroyed the rule of

law as it was understood in the eighteenth century by subjecting it to the whim of the living generation.

74. [William E. Auckland,] *Principles of Penal Law* (London, second edition, 1771), 3.

75. Morton J. Horwitz, "The Rule of Law: An Unqualified Human Good?," *Yale Law Journal*, 86 (1977): 566 (reviewing and quoting Thompson, *Hunters, supra* note 60). See also Robert W. Gordon, "Critical Legal Histories," *Stanford Law Review*, 36 (1984): 94. For comment, see Stephen B. Presser, "Some Realism About Orphism or the Critical Legal Studies Movement and the New Great Chain of Being: An English Legal Academic's Guide to the Current State of American Law," *Northwestern Law Review*, 79 (1985): 889-890.

76. See text to note 59, *supra*.

77. Perhaps we have already repudiated the legacy of the founders. The opposite of what the eighteenth century knew as liberty seems to be the guiding norm for "liberty" today. No longer can it be said, as it was in 1713, that "restraint of Government is the true *Liberty* and *Freedom* of the people," [Charles Leslie,] *The Right of Monarchy Asserted; Wherein the Abstract of Dr. King's Book, With the Motives for Reviving it at this Juncture are fully considered* (London, 1713), 18.

78. That is, an instrumentalism manifested by a judicial activism of such a nature that the voters of one American jurisdiction were recently moved to reject a state supreme court chief justice and two puisne justices. Compare the judicial theory of that state court to the judicial theory of the eighteenth century.

> The notion that an appellate judge, a servant of the state, might, in a particular matter, discover and articulate "the public interest" on his [or her] own, directly contradicted several tenets of colonial legal ideology. To eighteenth-century Whigs such effrontery might have been seen as a paradigm of arbitrary government.

Hendrik Hartog, "Conclusion," in *Law in the American Revolution and the Revolution in the Law—A Collection of Review Essays on American Legal History*, edited by Hendrik Hartog (New York, 1981), 242.

79. Although its critics might limit its validity to intraclass conflict:

> [T]he theory of the rule of law . . . expresses a vision of equality and individualism that is consistent with social relations within the dominated classes. Through its role as an arbiter whose neutrality is ordinarily apparent and frequently real, the state provides an ideological expression of the fragmentation of the dominated classes: if injustice occurs, recourse can be had to the neutral state and thus alternative institutions premised on ideas of solidity may be avoided.

Mark Tushnet, "Truth, Justice, and the American Way: An Interpretation of Public Law Scholarship in the Seventies," *Texas Law Review*, 57 (1979): 1350.

The Jeffersonian Republicans
and Civil Liberty

by Michael Les Benedict

As Americans celebrate the bicentennial of the framing and ratification of the Constitution of the United States and the Bill of Rights I perceive a danger: it is that we will honor our Constitution as part of the *iconography* of the nation, merely as a hollowed artifact to stir our national pride. Of course, the reader will anticipate the next sentence—that the Constitution is much more, that it is the guarantee of our liberties and the fundamental agreement wherein Americans have defined and limited governmental power. Yet it would be no more correct to celebrate the Constitution as the "guarantee of our liberties" than it would be to celebrate it merely as a symbol of our nationality. For the fact is, that wonderful document does *not* itself protect our liberties, nor even, as a practical matter, define what they are.

There are many nations that have constitutions that define and guarantee rights—that guarantee freedom of speech, of the press, and of assembly, for example. Some are even more liberal in their definitions and guarantees than ours, specifying that the government "shall guarantee its citizens freedom of speech, of the press, of meetings and assemblies," and even of "processions and demonstrations." That, as it happens, is article 83 of the constitution of Poland.

Evidently, a constitution itself does not guarantee liberty. What we must celebrate during the bicentennial is not merely the American Constitution but American *constitutionalism*, the commitment to the idea that to protect the liberty of the citizen, the fundamental law imposes limits upon democratic government that cannot be transgressed. In the absence of a national consensus upon that idea, a constitution is no more than what its name indicates, a document that sets up the institutional framework of government—that "constitutes" it. With the presence of such a commitment, one does not even need the document. The United Kingdom has a constitution, but one would look forever in the Public Records Office trying to find it. It is an unwritten constitution, made up of the customs and traditions of government that Englishmen believe to be fundamental.

Not only does the Constitution of itself not guarantee liberties, it cannot even be said really to define liberties. The Constitution does set down general principles of liberty. "Congress shall make no law . . . abridging the freedom of speech, or of the press," the Bill of Rights says, nor "shall cruel and unusual punishment be inflicted" (Amendments I and VII). But just what is this freedom of speech that must not be abridged? Just what punishments *are* "cruel and unusual"?

A simple answer, sensible at least over the past century, would be to say that the courts, especially the Supreme Court, answers these questions of definition. But that too would be misleading. Court decisions are only part of the process by which Americans define and protect liberty. The historian can look back and identify great constitutional decisions that really were made outside the courts—the decision to abolish slavery, for example, and the consequent definition of American citizenship and its rights, or the decision of the 1930s redefining "due process of law" so as to concede broad power to government to regulate economic matters. In fact, historians can look back and identify how court decisions themselves reflect political decisions, made by the mass of the American people, on issues that involved the definition of rights. It is not a novel observation to say that the constitutional law established by the Supreme Court since the 1930s reflects the social and economic understandings of American liberalism that triumphed in those years.[1] Nor, surely, have the more conservative decisions of the past fifteen years been unrelated to the revival of conservative social and economic understandings in society at large.

Americans have disagreed fundamentally about the nature of our society and the rights of individuals and groups within it. We have settled these disputes not by sending them to the courts for a kind of arbitration, but through the political process, in a series of political collisions that have shaped our concepts of rights and liberty. It is in those times of conflict that Americans set their constitutional compass.

The controversy between the Federalists and Jeffersonian Republicans was one of these collisions, and one of the most important that have shaped American rights and liberties. By the time it culminated in the crucial elections of 1800, the issues had been joined in such a way that in the opinion of most Americans the Republicans had become the party of liberty, while the Federalists had become the party of tyranny. And yet, with the hindsight of nearly two hundred years, we can see that this was too stark a distinction. Both Federalists and Republicans had inherited the republican ideology so pervasive in the Revolutionary era, but they diverged in their application of it. The struggle of the 1790s was between two different understandings of society and therefore of how best to secure liberty.

The first of these understandings we identify with Jefferson, Madison, George Mason, and others. They believed that efforts to promote intellectual conformity through governmental action was one of the great threats to liberty. Governments traditionally had tried to promote such conformity in the area of religion, for example. What had been the result? "To make one half the world fools, and the other half hypocrites," Jefferson scoffed. "It is error alone that needs the support of government. Truth can stand by itself."[2] Madison echoed him. "Religious bondage shackles and debilitates the mind." It "unfits it for every noble enterprise, every expanded project."[3] Thus efforts to enforce religious orthodoxy fit men for servitude. They prompted "pride and indolence in the Clergy, ignorance and servility in the laity; in both superstition, bigotry and persecution," hardly the material of republican liberty.[4]

The same convictions determined Jefferson's position on freedom of political expression. "[H]aving banished from our land that religious intolerance under which mankind so long bled and suffered, we have yet gained little if we countenance a political intolerance as despotic, as wicked, and as capable of as bitter and bloody persecutions," he would urge in his first inaugural address. Let those with even the most outrageous political opinions "stand undisturbed as monuments to the safety with which error of opinion may be tolerated where reason is left free to combat it."[5]

Closely related to Jefferson's and Madison's belief in toleration was their commitment to "equal rights" and "no special privileges." Among the problems with government efforts to impose political and religious beliefs was that they denied the equal right of each person to decide such questions for himself; or, as the Virginia Declaration of Rights of 1776 put it, every person was "equally entitled to the free exercise of Religion according to the dictates of conscience."[6] An established church was an even greater violation of the Jeffersonian injunction against special privileges, as was made clear by the language Madison proposed when he first tried unsuccessfully to disestablish Virginia's Episcopalian church: "that no man or class of men ought, on account of religion, to be connected with peculiar emoluments or privileges."[7] In sum, republican government "will be best supported by protecting every citizen in the enjoyment of his Religion with the same equal hand which protects his person and his property; and by not invading the equal rights of any Sect."[8] Jefferson, Madison, and other future Jeffersonian Republicans had put these beliefs into practice in Virginia: after a long struggle, they had disestablished the Episcopalian church with the passage in 1786 of the Virginia Statute for Establishing Religious Freedom.[9]

Equally committed to republican liberty, Federalists disagreed with what they considered extreme views of religious and political toleration and of equal rights. A community must establish a clear set of values and norms in order to maintain social harmony, they insisted. Thus Adams proposed in his inaugural address to support efforts "to encourage . . . every institution for propagating knowledge, virtue, and religion . . . as the only means of preserving our Constitution."[10] Of course, liberty required toleration of a moderate degree and amount of dissent; and so long as the institutions that promoted common values remained strong, only a moderate amount of dissent was likely. People would defer to traditional leaders and act according to established customs. But if each person had an equal right to assess the validity of institutions and customs according to his own reason, the consequence was likely to be extreme and widespread dissent, and this meant competition, conflict, and disorder. "When the minds of [the multitude] are loosened from their attachment to ancient establishment and courses, they seem to grow giddy and are apt . . . to run to anarchy," Alexander Hamilton worried.[11] Disagreement was likely to become intense and, ironically, toleration less likely. Federalists doubted the ability of ordinary people to restrain their passions in such circumstances; they would follow demagogues, who catered to their particular prejudices and interests. The result would be the tyrannical domination of one group over another, or else the defensive use of governmental power to suppress the agitators. As Fisher Ames put it, "[T]here may be . . . the least control and the most liberty there, where . . . the old habits and sober reason of the people . . . govern them. . . . [I]t is plain that those, whom manners and morals can no longer govern, must be governed by force."[12]

The Republican version of tolerance denied government the power to help sustain those institutions, especially the church, that promoted common moral standards. By leaving final decisions in matters of public and private morals to each individual, without clear guidance from any publicly sanctioned institutions, Jeffersonian Republican ideals seemed likely to destroy the very liberty they claimed to protect. Federalists cited as evidence the Terror inaugurated by the anticlerical demagoguery of the Jacobins in France. That was what came from a celebration of Reason over Authority—"a league . . . between the apostles and disciples of irreligion and anarchy," as Hamilton denounced the French Revolution.[13] Its excesses were a "bloody buoy, thrown out as a warning to the political pilots of America."[14]

Federalists perceived religious institutions as the chief promoters of proper values. Today we still debate whether the role of religious institutions in promoting community standards of moral behavior justify some government accommodation of them. Still, not even the most fervent New Right cleric suggests that the promotion of proper values requires the official establishment of a particular Christian denomination. But that was a common notion in the eighteenth century. "[A] religious establishment in a State is conducive to its peace and happiness," Episcopalian ministers petitioned the Virginia state assembly in 1776. "[I]t cannot be improper for the legislative body of a State to consider how such opinions as are most consonant to reason and of the best efficacy in human affairs may be propagated and supported, . . . and . . . these can be best taught and preserved in their purity in an established church."[15] "Religion makes men republicans," Federalists insisted, and "irreligion . . . contributes . . . to . . . destroy a community."[16] That is why in 1802 Hamilton proposed to save liberty, threatened by triumphant Republicanism, by creating "Christian Constitutional Societies."[17]

A sense of religious community, Federalists argued, promoted a general social balance and harmony that was essential to the maintenance of liberty. Alexander Hamiton despaired of maintaining such harmony, convinced that "all communities divide themselves into the few and the many," "the rich and well-born . . . [and] the mass of the people."[18] Recognize the melancholy truth, he urged, and shape government to give the elite a large voice so that it could restrain the multitude.[19] But in this he differed from most Federalists, who believed that liberty depended upon avoiding such divisions. As the Federalist governor of Massachusetts said in an address published in a collection revealingly titled *Patriotism and Piety*, "The strength of a republick consists in the mutual dependence and agreement of its several parts."[20] "Let the rich and the poor be united in the bonds of mutual affection," John Adams insisted. "A balance . . . must be preserved or liberty is lost forever."[21]

In a harmonious, united community leadership would devolve naturally upon those best fit for it—the most talented and capable whose abilities had already brought them success in private life. "[P]ick up the first 100 men you meet, and make a republic," Adams challenged Jefferson late in their lives. "Every man will have an equal vote. But when deliberations and discussions are opened, it will be found that 25 by their talents . . . will be able to carry 50 votes. Every one of these is an aristocrat, in my sense of the word."[22] Only the virtue of such leaders could protect liberty. Hamilton recalled with satisfaction how, "when Great Britain attempted to wrest from us those rights, without which we must have descended from the rank of freemen, . . . [the] mass and weight of talents, property, and character hastened to confederate in the public cause." That was how public life ought to be organized. Inspired by such leadership, "[t]he great body of our community everywhere . . . were eager to make sacrifices on the altar of their country."[23] Deference to such leadership must be encouraged. "[L]iberty . . . cannot exist without the habit of just subordination," Ames insisted. Republican notions of equality destroyed that habit. "All men being free and equal, rulers become our servants. . . . This generation, being equal to the last, owes no obedience to its institutions."[24]

Federalists believed that government must be framed to avoid the divisions that undermined liberty. "The only enemy which Republicanism has to fear in this country is the spirit of faction and anarchy," Hamilton wrote in 1792.[25] "Faction" had long been the bugbear of republican ideology. All had agreed that republics depended upon men putting aside narrow personal and group interests and acting for the welfare of the whole; those who manifested a contrary spirit endangered the entire republican enterprise.

This notion depended upon the belief that people could distinguish between honest disagreements over public policy, where people committed to the general good disagreed over particulars of how to secure it, and disagreements in which one side or both were motivated by a desire to secure particular interests. If only Americans "would withdraw their attachment from systems and name," Noah Webster lamented, "the sober, reflecting unambitious citizens of both parties would . . . coalesce on every measure essential to the public safety. If . . . they would investigate principles and understand the true interests of the United States, the great body of people would unite in their conclusions."[26] Republican thinkers knew that not everyone would agree at every occasion on how best to promote the public interest. But it was crucial that no organized, consistent opposition develop, for if it did the only explanation was that the divisions reflected rival interests, that one group or all were straying from the path of disinterested public virtue.[27]

So long as most Americans adhered to such a conviction political liberty remained tenuous, because it precluded full acceptance of the legitimacy of organized opposition in public affairs. Inevitably men *were* going to be influenced by their differing social backgrounds and economic interests when considering public questions, and they were going to arrive at different conclusions about just what was in the public interest. Just as inevitably, each side would be convinced that its conclusions embodied the public good, while its opponents' reflected corrupt self-interest.

By the 1790s Jeffersonian Republicans were coming to realize this. Madison had seen it as early as the 1780s. "As long as the reason of man continues fallible, . . . different opinions will be formed. As long as the connection subsists between his reason and his self-love, his opinions and his passions will have a reciprocal influence on each other. . . . The latent causes of faction are thus sown in the nature of man," he wrote in *The Federalist Number 10*.[28] But if, as Jefferson and Madison insisted, truth rather than force was the proper weapon with which to fight error, then factions must be tolerated. Of the alternative, Madison wrote, "[i]t could never be more truly said . . . of the . . . remedy, that it was worse than the disease."[29] Therefore Madison eschewed hope that the new Constitution of the United States would eliminate factions; it would rather reduce the likelihood of particular factions gaining control of the government.[30]

Hamilton did not share these perceptions. He told the New York ratifying convention that "[w]e are attempting by this Constitution to abolish factions and to unite all parties for the general welfare."[31] With their greater concern for maintaining harmony, their conviction that only the talented elite was capable of disinterested government, Federalists retained their old fear of factions in its fullest degree. Certain that they acted only for the public good, Federalists viewed Republicans as a mere faction, their leaders as dangerous demagogues, and their political organization illegitimate.[32]

So Federalists and Republicans presented to Americans quite divergent views about the meaning of liberty in the United States and how to preserve it. But Americans did not choose to support one party or the other purely on the abstract principles they represented. As in all such conflicts, it was the practical application of the principles that led people to determine where they stood.

Traditionally, historians have described the Federalist-Republican controversy in terms of the national issues which led to the clear party division: the Federalist's adoption of the Hamiltonian financial program, which strengthened the national government by having it assume the war debts of the states and refund its own debt at full value; their endorsement of his proposal to foster economic development through such national instruments as a protective tariff and a national bank; the maintenance of a standing national army and pursuance of a foreign policy sympathetic to Great Britain and hostile to newly republican France.

It is, of course, well known that by these policies Hamilton hoped to tie the interests of a variety of groups to the national government. "The true politician . . . takes human nature . . . as he finds it," Hamilton had concluded. "Our prevailing passions are ambition and interest; and it will ever be the duty of a wise government to avail itself of the passions, in order to make them subservient to the public good."[33] In his public reports he frankly avowed the benefits his proposals would provide to specific groups in the community. But ultimately Federalists were convinced their program would benefit the whole community, binding its elements more closely together and promoting that harmony essential to liberty and order. "Our interests when candidly considered are one," they insisted. What benefited the merchant or the mechanic ultimately benefited the farmer as well.[34]

But Republicans perceived government policies benefiting particular groups as violating the principle of "equal rights." A national bank, a protective tariff, a program to pay off state and national debts now in the hands of mere "speculators" instead of their original holders—all these proposals were designed to benefit a small, influential portion of the community at the expense of the rest, they complained. Taxes for such purposes were "arbitrary seizures of one class of citizens for the service of the rest." A protective tariff was a clear example: "[a] just security to property is not afforded by that government, under which unequal taxes oppress one species of property and reward another species," Madison insisted.[35]

Federalists' stress on the political primacy of the talented few, combined with policies that seemed to appeal to the special interests of the elite, appeared to warrant the accusation that they governed in the interest of an aristocracy. The Federalists "are more partial to the opulent than to the other classes of society," Republicans charged. "[H]aving debauched themselves, it follows with them, of course, that government can be carried on only by the pageanty of rank, the influence of money and emoluments, and military force." Inevitably, this was leading America toward the British model of government—one by corrupt influence, substituting the motive of private interest in place of public duty, converting its pecuniary dispensations into bounties to favorites or bribes to opponents, accommodating its measures to the avidity of a part of the nation instead of to the welfare of the whole.[36] To resist, Jeffersonians created Democratic and Republican Societies, dedicated "To support and perpetuate the EQUAL RIGHTS OF MAN," as the constitution of the New York Democratic Society affirmed.[37] In the rough-and-tumble of eighteenth-century polemic, the Federalists were the aristocratic, monarchical party. Their pro-British, anti-French Republic foreign policy confirmed the charge.

But Americans judged by more than the application of Federalist and Republican principles to national issues. Throughout the country people applied them to local conflicts, often of more immediate practical import than matters of national policy.

Perhaps the most widespread of these local conflicts was that over the proper relationship between church and state. The great Republican leaders, Jefferson and Madison, had already made clear the relevance of Republican principles to that issue in the most graphic way possible, by having led the movement to disestablish Virginia's Episcopalian church. More than that, they had frustrated the alternative proposal to establish *all* Virginia's Christian denominations by authorizing a state-enforced general assessment to be divided among them. That proposal had been made by their great political rival, Patrick Henry, and had been supported by John Marshall, by the 1790s both leading Federalists.[38]

North Carolina's history was similar to Virginia's. Despite the fact that dissenters were a majority in the colony, before the Revolution they were subject to the Schism Act, which excluded them from most public offices and positions in schools and seminaries. Permission to establish dissenting religious institutions and to worship freely was granted by the British Toleration Act, enforced in the colony, but the wide variety of discriminations against dissenting churches and privileges for the Anglican church had continued until the Revolution, when the new state constitution disestablished it. Yet conflict persisted over remaining special privileges, such as Episcopalian domination of the University of North Carolina, based on its old charter.[39] In Georgia the battle to disestablish the Episcopalian church did not end until 1798, when a new, Republican-sponsored state constitution incorporated a clause modeled after the Virginia Statute of Religious Liberty. The clause also ended state collection of a general assessment to support all religious denominations.[40]

The battles were more bitter in Connecticut and Massachusetts. In no state was an established church as well entrenched after the Revolution as the Congregationalist in Connecticut. Only in 1784 did Connecticut relieve dissenters from the obligation of paying assessments to support the established church, and it required them to sign formal certificates declaring their religious preference to do so. As the official church, Congregationalism received a variety of special privileges in the distribution of state funds for the support of schools. Baptists, Quakers, Episcopalians, and other dissenters joined in protest.[41] In Massachusetts and New Hampshire the struggles were nearly as bitter and victory for disestablishment would take even longer.[42] Even Vermont—where dissenters were tolerated to a far larger degree than in Connecticut, Massachusetts, and New Hampshire—experienced a series of sharp clashes before its Congregationalist church was disestablished in 1807.[43]

Closely related to the disestablishment struggles were efforts to repeal particular privileges secured by dominant churches, sometimes long after they were disestablished. In Virginia, for example, Episcopalian clerics tried to retain title to "glebe lands," donated by the colony to their support in earlier years, while Baptists, Presbyterians, and other formerly dissenting denominations urged the legislature to reclaim title over them and to eliminate all discriminatory legislation still on the statute books.[44] Former dissenters worked to undermine the control Episcopalians exercised over William and Mary College in Virginia and that which Congregationalists exercised at Harvard, Yale, and Dartmouth,[45] or to secure equal state support for their own institutions.[46]

Those who sought to disestablish official churches, or at least to secure more equitable treatment for dissenters, naturally turned to the party of "equal rights," whose leaders had disestablished the Episcopalian church in Virginia and were also known for their opposition to sectarian control of higher education.[47] They cited Republican opposition to "special privileges" as they sought to repeal the laws and charters that sanctioned them. The rhetoric of the struggle in Connecticut is instructive: grants voted to Congregationalist-dominated Yale College were inconsistent with the premise of "equal rights and privileges to Christians of every denomination," Connecticut dissenters complained.[48] Baptist elder Amos Wells entitled his address calling for disestablishment *The Equal Rights of Man Asserted.*[49] When Baptist elders in 1803 petitioned the legislature to repeal the requirement that dissenters present certificates in order to escape paying taxes to support the established church, they began, "Your petitioners believe that all mankind are entitled to equal rights and privileges, esp. the rights of conscience."[50] Attacking religious establishment in Connecticut, the radical clergyman John Leland, who precipitated the disestablishment movement there, paraphrased Jefferson: "Truth disdains the aid of law for its defence, . . . it will stand upon its own merit."[51] The Baptist petitioners echoed them both: "Truth has ever been most successful when left to combat error in the open field of argument and free discussion."[52]

Naturally, the relevance of Republican rhetoric led opponents of religious establishment and privilege to identify with Jefferson and Madison's party, while the party pledged itself to purge discrimination where it still existed. Almost everywhere, Republicans were identified with efforts to eliminate sectarian privilege.[53]

Just as naturally, those who perceived established churches, or at least state support for religious institutions generally, to be an essential bulwark of republican liberty and order turned to the Federalists. They blasted the Republicans, and particularly Jefferson, as atheists, whose success would "destroy religion, introduce immorality, and loosen the bonds of society."[54] They could not help but agree with Washington, who affirmed in his Farewell Address, largely drafted by Hamilton, that "religion and morality" were "indispensable supports" of "political prosperity," that religious inculcation of national morality was "the foundation of the fabric" of free government. They knew who Washington meant when he warned, "[i]n vain would that man claim the tribute of patriotism who should labor to subvert these great pillars of human happiness—these firmest props of the duties of men and citizens."[55] During the presidential election four years later, New Jersey Federalists put it more simply. The major issue was "GOD—AND A RELIGIOUS PRESIDENT; or JEFFERSON—AND NO GOD!!!"[56] Federalist denunciations of Deistic France resonated with the same concerns, as clerics in the established churches worried about the *French mania*—the "infidel and irreligious spirit"—and lambasted the Republicans for spreading it.[57]

Republican equal-rights rhetoric seemed applicable to disputes over control of land as well. In the Maine district of Massachusetts, settlers complained of the special influence through which absentee Massachusetts proprietors had secured title to millions of acres of undeveloped land. As proprietors withheld the land from the market, settlers simply began to carve out farms. Naturally, they reacted with fury when the proprietors began to send out surveyors and to demand that settlers purchase the now-improved land at inflated prices. Massachusetts Republicans quickly rallied to protect farmers from the rapacity of "mere speculators," whose wealth and influence had secured their titles in the first place. As dissenting religion also was stronger in this area than anywhere else in Massachusetts, the district of Maine soon became a Republican stronghold.[58]

In Georgia, the conflict was even sharper. There in 1795 a handsomely bribed Federalist legislature turned over millions of acres along the Yazoo River and its environs to a syndicate of Federalist land speculators. The reaction against this favoritism was immediate and overwhelming, destroying the Federalist party in the state. On securing control of the state government, the Republicans repealed the land sale and arranged a constitutional convention that disestablished the Episcopalian church and ended the system of general assessments to support religious institutions.[59] It is instructive to note the language of the repeal act, which resolved that the Yazoo law violated the principles of a "democratical . . . government founded on equality of rights, and which is totally opposed to all proprietary grants or monopolies in favor of a few, which tend to build up . . . aristocracy."[60]

In North Carolina the struggle was between small landholders and the Federalist-dominated University of North Carolina. To support higher education, the state legislature turned over to the university the claims against North Carolinians it had confiscated from Englishmen and Tories. When the university pressed these claims in the courts as vigorously as any Tory could, the outraged farmers secured the repeal of the laws, with the legislative votes following party lines.[61]

A similar issue arose when Federalists insisted that Tories, whose lands had been confiscated and sold during the Revolution, must be able to reclaim their property, as guaranteed by the Treaty of Paris, which ended the war. As the speculators, who had purchased Tory claims at depreciated prices, descended upon the good yeomen who had purchased confiscated property from their states, it seemed somehow that the undeserving had received the special favor of government. Once again Republicans took the lead in resisting the claims of the "speculators," while Federalists insisted that the Treaty be scrupulously observed.[62]

Yet another area where the Republican call for "equal rights" resonated concerned the social status and political influence of the growing American artisan class. Naturally, Republican attacks on Federalists' "aristocratic" leanings appealed to "honest mechanics," proud of their role in the Revolution and demanding recognition as valued members of society. And Federalist statements about the necessity of securing added influence in public affairs to a natural aristocracy of talent—meaning men of wealth and social position—were hardly likely to attract artisan support. Nor were calls upon them to defer to merchants, as their "natural patrons and friends."[63] But, as Howard B. Rock has observed in his study of New York artisans, it was at the local, "most vital and most apparent level that craftsmen saw their place in the community and their chapter in the national contest over the shape of American society at stake."[64]

Federalists displayed their conception of society, for example, when they staunchly defended property requirements in New York City elections. Republicans led the fight to remove "this aristocracy . . . from the metropolis of our state."[65] As Rock has summed up their argument, "[a]ll who had a stake in society, if only through their skills, should have an equal opportunity to decide who their leaders would be."[66] In a New York episode that was crucial in alienating artisans from the Federalist party, local Federalist judges railroaded two ferrymen who had got into an argument with a Federalist alderman. Denied counsel and the opportunity to answer the charges, the ferrymen were found guilty of insulting a government official. They were sentenced to two months at hard labor and, although in poor health, one of them was whipped, dying within a year. When a Republican lawyer petitioned the Federalist state assembly to impeach the judges and then criticized it in print for failing to do so, the assemblymen hailed the lawyer before the bar of the house and charged him with a breach of its privileges. Then it remanded him to jail to await trial by the assembly. That proceeding, conducted before the same body that charged him, became a *cause célèbre*, with crowds of Republican workingmen cheering their champion and denouncing his oppressors. In one event, acting on their own views of society, Federalists had managed to alienate workingmen, deprive defendants of fair trials, and attack freedom of speech and the press.[67]

It is within the context of all this that one must approach the Federalist passage of the Alien and Sedition Acts in 1798.[68] To men who were convinced that liberty depended upon harmony in the community and deference to natural leaders, to men convinced that faction posed mortal danger to republican government, to men who believed their opponents were acting in the interests of a foreign power, to men who believed support for religious institutions vital to republican morality and who perceived their opponents to be consciously undermining them, the Alien and Sedition Acts were not denials of liberty but measures essential to preserve it.

And they were in dead earnest. The Alien Act authorized the deportation, without trial, of leading political opponents: men such as Albert Gallatin, ranking Republican congressman and future Secretary of the Treasury, and Philip Freneau, editor of Jefferson's personal organ, the Philadelphia *National Gazette*. The Sedition Act was designed to shut down the opposition press at the approach of a presidential election.

Nothing could have illustrated more graphically the difference between the Federalist and the Republican understandings of liberty. But it was not the only illustration. It was rather the *final* illustration, not in the chronological sense but in the logical sense. As the elections of 1800 and after would show, to most Americans Republicans had become the defenders of equal rights, of religious freedom, of freedom of speech and the press, and of due process of law, while the Federalists, avowed friends of liberty, were perceived to be its enemy.[69]

When Republican orators, pamphleteers, and newspapers attacked their opponents as "aristocrats," "secret monarchists," and "crypto-Tories," and when they sloganeered "equal rights" and "no special privileges," they were compressing into catchwords a much more fully developed philosophy of rights in American society and presenting it to ordinary Americans in the most potent political terms they could. When Federalists called Republicans "atheists" and "Jacobins," they were doing the same. When a Massachusetts Baptist voted Republican, he may have been motivated primarily by spleen against that Congregationalist aristocracy in his state. The squatter on Georgia's Yazoo lands may have been voting Republican to keep his farm. But the party they were voting for stressed the general principle as much as, or more than, the specific abuse. It abstracted from specific circumstances general principles, and a political victory for it was a victory for the principles as well.

Republicans not only won the elections of 1800, over the next decade they became the overwhelmingly dominant party, with Federalists fading into oblivion even where they had once been strongest. The Alien and Sedition Acts were permitted to lapse. Despite the tenacity of limited common-law definitions of freedom of speech, prosecutions for seditious libel became fewer and fewer.[70] As they achieved power in the states, Republicans stripped particular religious denominations of their special privileges.[71] In state after state property qualifications for voting and holding office were repealed; in new ones, which Republicans controlled from the outset, they were never instituted.[72]

Americans had set their constitutional compass. The course was set in the direction of free speech, free press, separation of church and state, and equality as we have come to know them.

The Ohio State University

NOTES

1. The standard American constitutional history textbook makes the point, referring in a chapter title to the decisions of the Warren Court as "the culmination of New Deal liberalism," Alfred H. Kelly, Winfred A. Harbison, and Herman Belz, *The American Constitution: Its Origins and Development* (6th edition, New York, 1983), 635.

2. Thomas Jefferson, *Notes on the State of Virginia*, in Jefferson, *Writings*, selected by Merrill Peterson (New York, 1984), 286.

3. James Madison to William Bradford, 1 April 1774, in *The Papers of James Madison*, ed. William T. Hutchinson and William M. E. Rachal (15 vols., Chicago, 1962-1985), 1: 112-113.

4. Madison, *Memorial and Remonstrance Against Religious Assessments*, in Hutchinson and Rachal (eds.), *Papers of James Madison*, 8: 301.

5. James D. Richardson (comp.), *A Compilation of the Messages and Papers of the Presidents, 1789-1897* . . . (10 vols., Washington, D.C., 1896-1899), 1: 322.

6. Virginia Declaration of Rights, 1776, in Francis Newton Thorpe (comp.), *The Federal and State Constitutions, Colonial Charters & Other Organic Laws of the States, Territories, and Colonies Now or Hitherto Forming the United States of America* (7 vols., Washington, D.C., 1909), 7: 3814.

7. Irving Brant, *James Madison: The Virginia Revolutionist* (Indianapolis & New York, 1941), 245.

8. Madison, *Memorial and Remonstrance*, 302.

9. The best accounts are Thomas E. Buckley, *Church and State in Revolutionary Virginia, 1776-1787* (Charlottesville, Va., 1977); Hamilton J. Eckenrode, *Separation of Church and State In Virginia: A Study in the Development of the Revolution* (Richmond, 1910); and Anson Phelps Stokes, *Church and State in the United States* (3 vols., New York, 1950), 1: 366-394.

10. Richardson (comp.), *Messages and Papers of the Presidents*, 1: 231.

11. Alexander Hamilton to John Jay, 26 November 1775, in *The Papers of Alexander Hamilton*, ed. Harold C. Syrett (26 vols., New York, 1961-1979), 1: 176-177.

12. Fisher Ames, "The Republican II," in *Works of Fisher Ames, as Published by Seth Ames*, ed. W. B. Allen (2 vols., Indianapolis, 1983), 1: 90. For the Federalists' stress on the necessity of harmony and order to liberty, see James M. Banner, *To the Hartford Convention: The Federalists and the Origins of Party Politics in Massachusetts, 1789-1815* (New York, 1980), 26-28.

13. Hamilton, "Fragment on the French Revolution," in *The Works of Alexander Hamilton*, ed. Henry Cabot Lodge (9 vols., New York, 1885), 7: 375. Often the extreme partisanship of Federalists' attacks on Jacobin "atheism" obstructs a clear view of the principle underlying their criticism. For examples besides the forementioned, see Peter Porcupine [William Cobbett], *A Bone to Gnaw, for the Democrats* (Philadelphia, 1795) and *A Little Plain English, Addressed to the People of the United States . . .* (Philadelphia, 1795); Hamilton, "The Vindication No. 1," in Syrett (ed.), *Papers of Hamilton*, 11: 461-465; Ames, "Equality I," in Allen (ed.), *Works of Fisher Ames*, 1: 237-240; [Noah Webster], *The Revolution in France considered in Respect to its Progress and Effects* (New York, 1794). See also Page Smith, *John Adams* (2 vols., New York, 1962), 2: 831, 921; Richard M. Rollins, *The Journey of Noah Webster* (Philadelphia, 1980), 50-51, 77-82; Richard E. Welch, *Theodore Sedgwick, Federalist: A Political Portrait* (Middletown, Conn., 1965), 122-123; Richard Beeman, *Patrick Henry: A Biography* (New York, 1974), 110-114, 189; W. P. Cresson, *Francis Dana: A Puritan Diplomat at the Court of Catherine the Great* (New York, 1930), 348-354; Gary B. Nash, "The American Clergy and the French Revolution," *William and Mary Quarterly*, 22 (3rd ser.) (1965): 392-412. Nash points out that the orthodox American clergy did not discover their anti-Jacobinism until Deism and criticism of organized religion became major forces in American intellectual life in the mid-1790s.

14. [Cobbett], *The Bloody Buoy, Thrown Out as a Warning to the Political Pilots of America . . .* (Philadelphia, 1796).

15. Memorial of the Clergy of the Established Church in Virginia, 8 November 1776, in Charles F. James, *Documentary History of the Struggle for Religious Liberty in Virginia* (Lynchburg, Va., 1906), 76-77.

16. Jacob Ide (ed.), *The Works of Nathaniel Emmons, D.D.* (2 vols., Boston, 1842), 2: 246-247; David Tappan, quoted in J. Earl Thompson, Jr., "A Perilous Experiment: New England Clergymen and American Destiny, 1796-1826" (unpublished Ph.D. dissertation, Princeton University, 1966), 267. Note also Samuel Kendall, *Religion the Only Sure Basis of Free Governments . . .* (Boston, 1804). See Smith, *Adams*, 2: 1078; Clinton Rossiter, *Alexander Hamilton and the Constitution* (New York, 1964), 124; Banner, *To the Hartford Convention*, 26-27.

17. Hamilton to James A. Bayard, [16 to 21] April, 1802, in Syrett (ed.), *Papers of Alexander Hamilton*, 25: 605-610.

18. Max Farrand (ed.), *The Records of the Federal Convention of 1787* (3 vols., New Haven, Conn., 1911), 1: 299.

19. Farrand (ed.), *Records*, 1: 288-289, 299.

20. Caleb Strong, *Patriotism and Piety, the Speeches of his Excellency Caleb Strong, Esq. . . . from 1800 to 1807* (Newburyport, Mass., 1808), 156.

21. Adams, *Discourses on Davila*, in *The Works of John Adams, Second President of the United States*, ed. Charles Francis Adams (10 vols., Boston, 1850-1856), 6: 396.

22. Adams to Jefferson, 15 November 1813, in Lester J. Cappon (ed.), *The Adams-Jefferson Letters* (2 vols., Chapel Hill, N.C., 1959), 2: 398.

23. Alexander Hamilton, "The Stand: Part I," in John C. Hamilton (ed.), *The Works of Alexander Hamilton* (7 vols., New York 1850-1851), 7: 639.

24. Ames, "Equality VI," in Allen (ed.), *Works of Fisher Ames*, 1: 256; Ames, "Equality I," ibid., 239.

25. Hamilton to Edward Carrington, 26 May 1791, in Syrett (ed.), *Papers of Alexander Hamilton*, 11: 444.

26. Noah Webster, *On Being an American: Selected Essays, 1783-1828*, ed. Homer D. Babbidge, Jr. (New York, 1967), 125.

27. Gordon S. Wood, *The Creation of the American Republic, 1776-1787* (Chapel Hill, 1969), 57-61; John R. Howe, "Republican Thought and the Political Violence of the 1790s," *American Quarterly*, 19 (1967): 147-165.

28. Alexander Hamilton, James Madison, and John Jay, *The Federalist*, ed. Benjamin Fletcher Wright (Cambridge, Mass., 1961), 130-131.

29. *Federalist*, ed. Wright, 130.

30. Richard Hofstadter, *The Idea of a Party System: The Rise of Legitimate Opposition in the United States, 1780-1840* (Berkeley, 1969), 24-28, 54-68.

31. *Debates and Proceedings of the Convention of the State of New York, Assembled at Poughkeepsie on the 17th of June 1788 to deliberate on the Form of Federal Government recommended by the General Convention at Philadelphia* (New York, 1788), 83.

32. Hofstadter, *The Idea of a Party System*, 86-111; Howe, "Republican Thought and the Political Violence of the 1790s," 158-160.

33. Hamilton, "Defence of the Funding System," in Lodge (ed.), *Works of Hamilton*, 7: 396. See Lance Banning, *The Jeffersonian Persuasion: Evolution of a Party Ideology* (Ithaca, N.Y., 1978), 129-140; Clinton Rossiter, *Alexander Hamilton and the Constitution* (New York, 1964), 128-137.

34. Theophilus Parsons, *Result of the Convention of Delegates Holden at Ipswich in the County of Essex* (Newburyport, Mass., 1778), 11-12. Parsons expressed this conviction in the 1770s, but it seems central to his later Federalism.

35. Madison, "Property," in Hutchinson and Rachal (eds.), *Papers of James Madison*, 14: 266-268.

36. Madison, "A Candid State of Parties," *Papers*, 14: 370-372; Banning, *The Jeffersonian Persuasion*, 141-160, 170-178; Drew R. McCoy, *The Elusive Republic: Political Economy in Jeffersonian America* (Chapel Hill, 1980), 152-161.

37. *Constitution of the Democratic Society of the City of New York* (New York, 1794).

38. Buckley, *Church and State in Revolutionary Virginia*, passim; Stokes, *Church and State in the United States*, 1: 366-397.

39. Stokes, *Church and State in the United States*, 1: 397-404.

40. Reba Carolyn Strickland, *Religion and the State in Georgia in the Eighteenth Century* (New York: 1939), 161-167.

41. Stokes, *Church and State in the United States*, 1: 408-418; Joseph Francis Thorning, *Religious Liberty in Translation: A Study of the Removal of Constitutional Limitations on Religious Liberty as Part of the Social Progress in the Transition Period* (Washington, D.C., 1931), 93-136; William G. McLoughlin, *New England Dissent, 1630-1833: The Baptists and Separation of Church and State* (2 vols., Cambridge, Mass., 1971), 2: 915-1062.

42. Stokes, *Church and State in the United States*, 1: 418-427; Thorning, *Religious Liberty in Transition*, 9-92, 143-192; McLoughlin, *New England Dissent*, 2: 833-911, 1065-1262; Jacob C. Meyer, *Church and State in Massachusetts From 1740 to 1833: A Chapter in the History of the Development of Individual Freedom* (Cleveland, 1930).

43. McLoughlin, *New England Dissent*, 2: 789-812.

44. Eckenrode, *Separation of Church and State in Virginia*, 116-161; Thomas E. Buckley, "Evangelicals Triumphant: The Baptist Assault on the Virginia Glebes, 1786-1801," *William and Mary Quarterly*, 45 (3rd ser. 1988): 36-69.

45. McLoughlin, *New England Dissent*, 883-895 (Dartmouth), 1027-1032 (Yale), 1184-1185 (Harvard); John S. Whitehead, *The Separation of College and State: Columbia, Dartmouth, Harvard and Yale, 1776-1876* (New Haven, 1973), 27-29 (Columbia), 41-45 (Yale); *Journal of the Debates and Proceedings in the Convention of Delegates Chosen to Revise the Constitution of Massachusetts, . . . 1820 . . . to 1821* (Boston, 1853), 69-87, 491-493, 527-533, 549-551 (Harvard); Meyer, *Church and State in Massachusetts*, 187-191 (Harvard); Greene, *Development of Religious Liberty in Connecticut*, 378-80 (Yale); Charles E. Cunningham, *Timothy Dwight, 1752-1817* (New York, 1942), 341-342 (Yale); Francis N. Stites, *Private Interest and Public Gain: The Dartmouth College Case, 1819* (Amherst, Mass., 1971), 10-22; Stephen J. Novak, "The College in the Dartmouth College Case: A Reinterpretation," *New England Quarterly*, 47 (1974): 550-563 (although in fact the struggle to control Dartmouth was between evangelical and non-evangelical Congregationalists and Presbyterians, the non-evangelicals recruited the Republicans to their cause by charging that their enemies were turning Dartmouth into a narrowly sectarian school); David C. Humphrey, *From King's College to Columbia* (New York, 1976), 279-282; Sadie Bell, *The Church, the State, and Education in Virginia* (Philadelphia, 1930), 170-204; Robert Polk Thompson, "The Reform of the College of William and Mary, 1763-1780," *Proceedings of the American Philosophical Society*, 115 (1971): 187-213, esp. 207-213. After it secured special state benefits, Virginians also tried to secularize Presbyterian Liberty College (later Washington and Lee). James Morrison Hutchinson, "Virginia's 'Dartmouth College Case,' " *Virginia Magazine of History and Biography*, 51 (1943): 134-140; Bell, *Church, State, and Education in Virginia*, 230-234.

46. McLoughlin, *New England Dissent*, 1122-1126; Thorning, *Religious Liberty in the Transition Period*, 100-106.

47. Jefferson had long worked to reduce sectarian control at William and Mary and had led the fight to establish the University of Virginia as a nonsectarian institution. Richard Hofstadter and Walter P. Metzger, *The Development of Academic Freedom in the*

United States (New York, 1955), 238-242; Gordon E. Baker, "Thomas Jefferson and Academic Freedom," *Bulletin of the AAUP*, 39 (1953): 377-387; Philip Alexander Bruce, *History of the University of Virginia, 1819-1919: The Lengthened Shadow of One Man* (5 vols., New York, 1920), 1: 17-24, 45-94. Buckley, "Evangelicals Triumphant," 56-57.

48. Thorning, *Religious Liberty in the Transition Period*, 100.

49. Wells, *The Equal Rights of Man Asserted* (Norwich, Conn., 1800).

50. Remonstrance and Petition of a Convention of Elders and Brethren of the Baptist Denomination Assembled at Bristol on the first Wednesday of February, 1803, in the *American Mercury*, 14 July 1803, p. 1.

51. John Leland, *The Rights of Conscience Inalienable, and, Therefore, Religious Opinions Not Cognizable By Law; Or, The High-Flying Churchman, Stripped of his Legal Robe, Appears a Yaho*, in Leland, *The Writings of Elder John Leland . . .* (New York, 1845), 185.

52. Remonstrance and Petition, in the *American Mercury*, 14 July 1803, p. 1.

53. For the politics of religious conflict in New England, see William A. Robinson, *Jeffersonian Democracy in New England* (New Haven, 1916), 128-150; Thorning, *Religious Liberty in Transition*, 42-63, 79-83, 100-137, 167, 172-193; Greene, *Religious Liberty in Connecticut*, 393-496; Meyer, *Church and State in Massachusetts*, 133-159. The link between Republicanism and the confiscation of the Episcopalian glebe lands, the final victory for dissenters over the established church in Virginia, is implicit but clear in Eckenrode, *Separation of Church and State in Virginia*, 144-145. In New York, with Protestant rivalries settled by disestablishment in the wake of the Revolution, Republicans championed the cause of Catholics seeking the right to hold political office, while Federalists once again opposed liberalization. John Webb Pratt, *Religion, Politics, and Diversity: The Church-State Theme in New York History* (Ithaca, N.Y., 1967), 122-129. For the Republican-led efforts to reduce the influence of favored denominations over state-aided colleges in Massachusetts, Connecticut, New Hampshire, New York, and Virginia, see the sources cited in note 40 above. See also Whitehead, *The Separation of College and State*, 16-21, 53-76 and Bruce A. Campbell, "The Dartmouth College Case as a Civil Liberties Case: The Formation of Constitutional Policy," *Kentucky Law Journal*, 70 (1980-1981): 670-695. Campbell suggests that the University of North Carolina got into trouble with the Republican legislature in part because many North Carolinians resented Presbyterian dominance there, ibid., 687-688.

54. Anonymous, *Serious Considerations on the Election of a President: Addressed to the Citizens of the United States* (New York, 1800), quoted in Charles O. Lerche, Jr., "Jefferson and the Election of 1800: A Case Study in the Political Smear," *William and Mary Quarterly*, 5 (1948): 474. Theophilus Parsons called Jefferson "the great archpriest of Jacobinism and infidelity," Parsons to John Jay, 5 May 1800, in Jay, *The Correspondence and Public Papers of John Jay*, ed. Henry P. Johnston (4 vols., New York, 1893), 4: 270. Hamilton denounced him privately as "an *atheist* in Religion and a *fanatic* in Politics," Hamilton to Jay, 7 May, 1800, ibid., 271.

55. Richardson (comp.), *Messages and Papers of the Presidents*, 1: 220.

56. Carl E. Prince, *New Jersey's Jeffersonian Republicans: The Genesis of an Early Party Machine, 1789-1817* (Chapel Hill, 1964), 60.

57. Nash, "The American Clergy and the French Revolution," 392-412, quoting William H. Channing at 403.

58. Paul Goodman, *The Democratic-Republicans of Massachusetts: Politics in a Young Republic* (Cambridge, Mass., 1964), 125-127.

59. C. Peter Magrath, *Yazoo: Law and Politics in the New Republic: The Case of Fletcher v. Peck* (Providence, R.I., 1966), 1-19; Albert Berry Saye, *A Constitutional History of Georgia, 1732-1945* (Athens, Ga., 1948), 147-162.

60. U.S. Congress, *American State Papers: Documents Legislative and Executive of the Congress of the United States . . . — Class VIII, Public Lands* (7 vols., Washington, D.C., 1832-1860), 1: 156-158 (quoted at 156). As late as 1814 the issue divided Federalists and Republicans, with the former supporting and most of the latter opposing a congressional appropriation to compensate Yazoo land speculators who had bought titles from the original crooks. Charles Grove Haines, *The Role of the Supreme Court in American Government and Politics, 1789-1835* (Berkeley and Los Angeles, 1944), 322-323.

61. Kemp P. Battle, *History of the University of North Carolina from Its Beginning to the Death of President Swain, 1789-1868* (2 vols., Raleigh, N.C., 1907), 1: 136-145, 155-158; Campbell, "The Dartmouth College Case," 687-688.

62. In litigation in Virginia, John Marshall had represented litigants claiming Tory-based titles and had himself speculated in Tory claims, while opponents included future Republican leaders Edmund Randolph and John Taylor of Caroline. Later litigation before the United States Supreme Court led to a confrontation between the Court and the Virginia Republican establishment, led by Virginia Chief Justice Spencer Roane. Albert Beveridge, *Life of John Marshall* (4 vols., Boston, 1916-1919), 4: 145-167; Leonard Baker, *John Marshall: A Life in Law* (New York, 1974), 293-298, 573-581; Henry F. Simms, *Life of John Taylor: The Story of a Brilliant Leader in the Early Virginia State Rights School* (Richmond, 1932), 39-40; Nicholas Pendleton Mitchell, *State Interests in American Treaties: A Study in the Making and Substantive Content of Certain International Agreements* (Richmond, Va., 1936), 117-120; William W. Crosskey, *Politics and the Constitution in the History of the United States* (2 vols., Chicago, 1953), 2: 785-817; George Lee Haskins and Herbert A. Johnson, *Foundations of Power: John Marshall, 1801-15*, Volume II of the Oliver Wendell Holmes Devise *History of the Supreme Court of the United States* (New York, 1981), 357-365, 502-506, 511-517.

63. Howard B. Rock, *Artisans of the New Republic: The Tradesmen of New York City in the Age of Jefferson* (New York, 1979), 47.

64. Rock, *Artisans*, 46.

65. New York *American Citizen*, 28 October 1801, quoted Rock, *Artisans*, 58.

66. Rock, *Artisans*, 50.

67. Alfred F. Young, *The Democratic Republicans of New York: The Origins, 1763-1797* (Chapel Hill, N.C., 1967), 476-493.

68. U.S. Congress, *The Public Statutes at Large of the United States of America . . .* (Boston, 1948), 1: 570-572, 596-597.

69. The literature on the Alien and Sedition Acts is voluminous. For the best general accounts of the laws and the response to them, see Leonard Levy, *Emergence of a Free Press* (New York, 1985), 297-338; Donald H. Stewart, *The Opposition Press of the Federalist Period* (Albany, 1969), 465-486; James Morton Smith, *Freedom's Fetters: The Alien and Sedition Laws and American Civil Liberties* (Ithaca, N.Y., 1956); John C. Miller, *Crisis in Freedom: The Alien and Sedition Acts* (Boston, 1952).

70. Alfred H. Kelly, "Constitutional Liberty and the Law of Libel: An Historian's View," *American Historical Review*, 74 (1968): 433. It should be noted that the decline of prosecutions for seditious libel did not follow immediately upon Jeffersonian political victories. Rather, it was implicit in Jeffersonian concepts of how to find truth and of free speech. See Levy, *Emergence of a Free Press*, 338-349; Richard Buel, Jr., "Freedom of the Press in the American Revolution: The Evolution of Libertarianism, 1760-1820," in Bernard Bailyn and John B. Hench (eds.), *The Press & the American Revolution* (Boston, 1981), 88-97.

71. Thorning, *Religious Liberty in Transition*, 42-63, 79-83, 100-137, 167, 172-193; Greene, *Religious Liberty in Connecticut*, 393-496; Meyer, *Church and State in Massachusetts*, 133-159; Campbell, "The Dartmouth College Case," 670-695.

72. Kirk H. Porter, *A History of Suffrage in the United States* (Chicago, 1918), 20-46; Marchette Chute, *The First Liberty: A History of the Right to Vote in America, 1619-1850* (New York, 1969), 279-305; Chilton Williamson, *American Suffrage: From Property to Democracy, 1760-1860* (Princeton, 1960), 138-222.

Liberty and Slavery in Early American Foreign Policy

by Don E. Fehrenbacher

Patrick Henry is no doubt best remembered today for the seven words with which he supposedly concluded his fiery address to a Virginia convention in March 1775. "Is life so dear, or peace so sweet," he asked, "as to be purchased at the price of chains and slavery? Forbid it, Almighty God—I know not what course others may take; but as for me, give me liberty, or give me death." He had begun the speech in much the same way, telling the convention that what it faced was "nothing less than a question of freedom or slavery." Later on, just before his peroration, he declared: "There is no retreat but in submission and slavery! Our chains are forged. Their clanking may be heard on the plains of Boston!"[1]

Clearly, the choice with which Henry importuned his fellow Virginians was not between liberty and death, but rather between liberty (at the risk of death) *and* political enslavement. Of course, the eloquent phrasing must be attributed in no small part to the literary skill and even the imagination of Henry's biographer, William Wirt, who reconstructed the speech from pretty thin evidence. But Wirt was well acquainted with the rhetoric of the Revolution, and there is a convincing verisimilitude in Henry's repeated juxtaposing of liberty and slavery. The metaphor of colonial argument against British imperial policy was frequently drawn from the realities of the slave system. For instance, George Washington in 1774 accused the British of "endeavouring by every piece of art and despotism to fix the shackles of slavery" upon the American people. "We must assert our rights," he warned, "or submit to every imposition that can be heaped upon us, till custom and use shall make us as tame and abject slaves as the blacks we rule over with such arbitrary sway."[2]

Such language, though used throughout the colonies, had special force in the South, where its images reflected everyday life.[3] There, the relation of liberty and slavery was something deeper than rhetoric and more complex than antithesis. Historians M. I. Finley and Orlando Patterson have suggested that the very concept of freedom emerged in the ancient world out of experience with slavery—that slavery thus in a sense created freedom.[4] Similarly, Edmund S. Morgan finds a symbiotic relationship between slavery and freedom in eighteenth-century Virginia. It was, he argues, the stability and social solidarity produced by the slaveholding system that enabled plantation aristocrats like Washington and Jefferson to become republicans and revolutionists.[5]

Chattel slavery in a nation explicitly dedicated to human freedom was a heritage both paradoxical and dangerous for the new United States. The domestic consequences of that heritage became the central theme of nineteenth-century American history, as increasing sectional conflict led eventually to disunion, civil war, and the aftermath called reconstruction. Less familiar are the effects of the heritage upon American foreign relations and upon the image of itself that the United States presented to the rest of the world.

American victory in the Revolutionary War meant that the abstract principles of the Declaration of Independence had been successfully converted into an actual experiment in nation-building. It made the new United States an international symbol, not only of revolutionary escape from alien rule, but of republican self-government and personal freedom. "The example of political wisdom and felicity here to be displayed will excite emulation through the kingdoms of the earth, and meliorate the condition of the human race." So spoke Joel Barlow in 1787,[6] and the same kind of gleam was in George Bancroft's eye many years later when he declared: "Our country is bound to allure the world to freedom by the beauty of its example."[7] Freedom was the keynote. Liberty personified as a young woman soon emerged as one of the earliest symbols of American nationhood. At the beginning of the Revolution, Tom Paine had pictured freedom as "hunted round the globe" and finding her last refuge on the American shore.[8] For many a European liberal, the struggle quickly took on similar meaning. *America* and *liberty*, says one European historian, "became interchangeable terms."[9]

Proud of their own Revolution, Americans of the early national period were deeply interested in other revolutionary movements that seemed to pay them the flattery of imitation. First, of course, came the great upheaval in France, which inspired passionate renewals of the commitment to freedom in the United States. Throughout the country, local societies sprang up in support of the French revolutionary cause, issuing public appeals such as the following: "Shall we Americans, who have kindled the spark of liberty, stand aloof and see it extinguished, when burning a bright flame, in France, which hath caught it from us? . . . Let us unite with France, and stand or fall together."[10] So much was at stake, said Thomas Jefferson in January 1793, that he would rather see "half the earth desolated" than the French Revolution crushed.[11]

Certain conservatives like John Adams were skeptical from the beginning, however, and by 1793, the excesses of violence in France had alienated many more. The wars of the French Revolution divided the country into bitterly hostile factions that soon took more definite form as the Federalist and Republican parties. Considerations of national interest and commercial welfare predominated in the shaping of public policy, but ideology was also a factor. For the better part of a decade, American foreign relations and domestic politics were strongly affected by the disposition of the emerging Jeffersonian Republicans to look upon embattled France as the old world's champion of political liberty in the tradition of the American Revolution.

Such views fell out of fashion, of course, with the rise of Napoleon Bonaparte to supreme power in France, but soon there were other revolutions to celebrate, as the Spanish colonial empire began to fall apart. Henry Clay, then Speaker of the House of Representatives, became the leading advocate of the revolutionary republics in South America, urging their early recognition by the United States. Predicting that the new nations would erect free governments animated by "an American feeling," he went on to say: "We [are] their great example. . . . They [have] adopted our principles, copied our institutions, and, in some instances, employed the very language and sentiments of our revolutionary papers."[12]

President James Monroe was cautiously disposed to favor recognition, but Secretary of State John Quincy Adams counseled delay, and his will prevailed. Not until 1822, with Florida safely transferred to the United States and Spain's rebellious colonies plainly beyond all hope of reconquest, did Monroe formally propose recognition and secure congressional approval.[13] A year later, in his instructions to the newly-appointed minister to Colombia, Adams wrote: "The principles upon which the right of independence has been maintained by the South American patriots have been approved, not only as identical with those upon which our own independence was asserted and achieved, but as involving the whole theory of Government on the emphatically American foundation of the sovereignty of the people and the unalienable rights of man."[14]

By that time, still another revolutionary movement had aroused much sympathy in the United States. The revolt of Greece against Turkish rule was bound to have special meaning for the people of a republic dedicated to liberty, and one local Greek assembly struck just the right note in an appeal for help addressed to the American people. "Having formed the resolution to live or die for freedom," the document began, "we are drawn toward you by a just sympathy; since it is in your land that Liberty has fixed her abode, and by you that she is prized as by our fathers. Hence, in invoking her name, we invoke yours at the same time, trusting that in imitating you, we shall imitate our ancestors, and be thought worthy of them if we succeed in resembling you."[15] The Greek cause had a number of well-known sponsors in the United States. It was warmly espoused by Albert Gallatin, for example, and it inspired eloquent speeches in the House of Representatives by Daniel Webster and Henry Clay.[16] Privately, Americans responded with generous contributions of money and supplies. Officially, the American government aided the Greek revolution only with words of encouragement. President Monroe, in several of his annual messages to Congress, expressed the hope that Greece would win its freedom, but otherwise, in accordance with the principles of the Monroe Doctrine, his administration adhered strictly to a policy of nonintervention. Congress refused to appropriate any money even for the relief of famine and destitution in Greece. The United States recognized Greek independence only after it had been guaranteed by the major European powers in 1833.[17]

Meanwhile, Americans had been moderately stirred by the Revolution of 1830 in France, which, although it merely liberalized the French monarchy, was labeled "a struggle for the sacred principles of liberty" by President Andrew Jackson.[18] Much more thrilling were the revolutions that swept across much of Europe in 1848. Americans sympathized especially with the efforts of submerged nationalities to free themselves from Austrian rule. In 1849, the United States sent an agent to Hungary armed with authority to recognize its revolutionary government if the circumstances seemed opportune, but conservative forces were already getting the upper hand in Hungary and elsewhere.[19] Americans watched with bitter disappointment as revolutionary movements collapsed in one country after another. Even France soon exchanged its newly-established Second Republic for the imperial reign of a new Napoleon.

The Austrian government lodged a formal protest against American interference in its domestic affairs and received a defiant reponse from Secretary of State Daniel Webster. "When the people of the United States behold the people of foreign countries . . . moving toward the adoption of institutions like their own," he wrote, "it surely cannot be expected of them to remain wholly indifferent spectators." Speaking a year later, at a banquet honoring Louis Kossuth, the Hungarian revolutionary leader, Webster declared, "We shall rejoice to see our American model upon the Lower Danube and on the mountains of Hungary." He concluded by offering a toast to Hungarian independence.[20]

In the Senate, Isaac P. Walker of Wisconsin went so far as to question whether the isolationism of earlier years was any longer appropriate. "What was our policy in our infancy and weakness, has ceased to be our *true* policy now that we have reached to manhood and strength," he declared. "I am for the cause of liberty and free Government, against slavery and despotism, throughout the globe." In support of that cause he was prepared to have the United States "interpose both her moral and physical power."[21] Such extravagant talk did not make much headway, however, against the traditional view of the nation's appointed role in world history. A Tennessee congressman spoke for most Americans when he dismissed all thought of intervention in Europe. With respect to Kossuth he declared: "It was our example which animated him and his Hungarians to the great and glorious efforts which they made. . . . [W]e will keep that light of our example burning and shining upon the pathway of nations . . . to guide them from the darkness of tyranny and despotism to the sunlight of liberty."[22]

The aggressiveness of Webster and Walker reflected the self-confidence of a nation that had recently expanded to the shores of the Pacific, adding more than a million square miles to its domain and reinforcing its conviction of having been born to a special destiny. Not surprisingly, some of the rhetoric of the time linked territorial expansion with the American ideal of liberty. Particularly in discussions of the annexation of Texas, expansion was often justified as a means of "extending the area of freedom." But this phrase, repeated until it became a cliché, was invested with a terrible irony; for, as an Indiana congressman bitterly complained, this "nation boasting itself to be the freest upon the earth" was being asked "to extend the area of freedom by enlarging the boundaries of slavery."[23]

The United States at mid-century was still viewed throughout much of the world as a symbol of personal liberty and self-government. Yet it had also come to be conspicuous as one of the last strongholds of slavery in western civilization. At home, the American nation was, of course, a house increasingly divided by the slavery question, but in the conduct of foreign affairs it appeared consistently as a slaveholding republic. Meanwhile, that old enemy Britain, the very epitome of oppression in Revolutionary rhetoric, had assumed the role of an international champion of human freedom. It was a British foreign minister who declared in 1843 that his country was "constantly exerting herself to procure the general abolition of slavery throughout the world." And it was an American secretary of state who responded with a vehement defense of slavery, which ended in the assertion that for his country, abolition would be a great "calamity."[24]

This inversion of the standard Revolutionary roles had actually begun during the Revolution, when slaves in large numbers sought freedom within British lines. At American insistence, the treaty of peace included a provision that the British forces must withdraw from the United States without "carrying away any Negroes or other Property of the American Inhabitants."[25] By that wording, the treaty explicitly recognized slaves as property, something the framers of the Constitution would studiously avoid. But the clause proved ineffective. Washington himself was unable to prevent the departure of some four thousand blacks with the British evacuation of New York City, and there were similar losses elsewhere.[26] What remained to disturb Anglo-American diplomacy for many years was the question of compensation.

After the Revolution, the United States government energetically pressed the claims of American slaveholders against Great Britain. The principal government spokesmen were John Adams, Gouverneur Morris, John Jay, and Thomas Jefferson—all men of antislavery convictions. But antislavery was then just a moral sentiment while slavery was an economic interest and, in the day-to-day conduct of public business, an interest will usually have the advantage. Besides, the issue of the appropriated slaves involved other principles important to Americans, including property rights of individuals and treaty rights of the nation.

Both Great Britain and the United States failed to meet all their obligations under the treaty of peace, and reproaches on the subject were duly exchanged for more than a decade. Americans protested especially against the British refusal to evacuate certain military posts situated on American soil. The British replied that the posts were being held in reprisal for American delinquencies with respect to Loyalists and British creditors. To which Jefferson, Jay, and others responded that the British had been the first to violate the treaty by carrying off the American slaves.[27]

Anglo-American relations deteriorated further when Britain went to war against Revolutionary France in 1793 and began to interfere with American maritime commerce. The situation soon became critical, and in 1794 President Washington sent Chief Justice John Jay to London as a special envoy seeking to resolve the differences between the two countries. Southerners suspected that Jay, a confirmed Anglophile and a friend of abolition, would not be very resolute in protecting their interests, and sure enough, he signed a treaty that said nothing about compensation for the carried-off slaves. This omission was a major reason for the bitter southern opposition to the treaty that almost defeated it in the Senate. Even after senatorial approval, James Madison led an attempt in the House of Representatives to strangle the treaty by withholding the appropriation necessary for carrying it into effect. The slave issue was prominent in a furious debate that ran on for two months before the effort finally failed.[28]

The United States never did obtain satisfaction from Britain for the slaves carried off during the Revolution. What is more, the same problem arose after the war of 1812. Several thousand Negroes were taken away from the Chesapeake region by the British fleet, in violation of an explicit provision in the treaty of peace.[29] Again the British government refused either to return the slaves or to indemnify the owners. This time there was a different outcome, however. John Quincy Adams, the American minister in London, pressed the issue so persistently that British officials at last agreed to submit it to arbitration.[30] Alexander I of Russia was eventually selected as the arbitrator. Adams, who by then had become secretary of state, found "something whimsical in the idea that the United States and Great Britain, both speaking English, should go to the Slavonian Czar of Muscovy to find out their own meaning, in a sentence written by themselves."[31] The czar ruled in favor of the American slaveholders, and, after further extensive negotiations about the details, the British in 1826 finally agreed to pay an indemnity of approximately $1,200,000.[32]

Meanwhile, federal officials wrestled with another perennial problem—that of slaves escaping across international boundaries to the north and south. For instance, slaveholders in Georgia had complained ever since the end of the Revolution that Spanish Florida was a haven for runaways. President Washington and his first secretary of state, Thomas Jefferson, expended considerable effort securing an agreement with Spanish officials for the return of fugitive slaves, but it was never adequately enforced.[33] After the war of 1812, slaveholders in Georgia and Alabama felt additionally threatened when several hundred militant blacks took possession of a fort lying within the Spanish jurisdiction on the Apalachicola River. The commander of American troops in the area received emphatic instructions on the subject from his superior officer. "If the fort harbours the Negroes of our citizens . . . or hold[s] out inducements to the slaves of our citizens to desert from their owners' service," wrote General Andrew Jackson, "this fort must be destroyed."[34] And destroyed it was. Two American naval vessels making their way up the river were fired upon from the fort and returned the fire. A hot shot struck the fort's powder magazine, and in the resulting explosion, nearly all of the occupants—men, women, and children—were killed outright or mortally wounded.[35] The officer reporting the bloody event to the secretary of the navy expressed satisfaction at this elimination of a "rendezvous for runaway slaves" that would have been "highly injurious to the neighboring states."[36]

Soon the cession of Florida to the United States erased the international boundary that had been so attractive to fugitives. Farther west, however, slaves could escape from Louisiana by crossing the Sabine River into Mexico, where slavery had been abolished. In 1827, with Adams now president and Henry Clay, secretary of state, the American minister to Mexico, Joel R. Poinsett, negotiated a commercial treaty with an article providing for the return of runaway slaves. But the article was rejected by both houses of the Mexican Congress, and the treaty eventually ratified contained no reference to the subject.[37] After the annexation of Texas and the war with Mexico, the problem shifted southwestward to the new international border at the Rio Grande. Several disturbances in that region during the 1850s were caused in part by fugitive slaves and some highhanded Texas efforts to recover them. Under pressure from Texas, the United States government sought an extradition treaty with Mexico that would include the return of fugitive slaves, but the negotiations failed.[38]

It was to Canada, however, that the largest number of slaves fled from the United States, and, beginning with John Quincy Adams, one secretary of state after another tried to make arrangements for orderly recovery of such fugitives. The standard response was the one given to Adams by the British chargé d'affaires in Washington when he declared: "The Negroes have, by their residence in Canada, become free, whatever may have been their former condition in this Country."[39] There remained the hope that at least those fugitives accused of crimes could be extradited, but Canadian officials nearly always found good reason to refuse extradition of a slave.[40] And so the United States government failed in its strenuous efforts virtually to extend the operation of American fugitive-slave legislation across international boundaries into Mexico and Canada.

Another kind of escape from slavery began to cause trouble in the early 1830s. Several coastwise vessels carrying slaves were shipwrecked in the British West Indies or forced by bad weather to seek shelter there. In each instance, colonial officials set the slaves free, provoking angry protests from all over the South. The state department and its spokesmen in London repeatedly demanded compensation for the slave-owners. One minister to England, a Virginian named Andrew Stevenson, dispatched letters of thirty, forty, and even fifty pages to Lord Palmerston, lecturing him on every aspect of the issue. Under the American Constitution, he declared, there was "no distinction in principle between property in persons and property in things." Domestic slavery was "infused" into the laws of the United States and mixed "with all the sources of their authority."[41] In the end, Stevenson managed to win a partial victory. The British government agreed to make restitution of about $115,000 for slaves liberated before 1833, the year in which Parliament passed the West Indian Emancipation Act.[42]

Soon, however, there came another event to infuriate southerners and disturb Anglo-American relations. In 1841, a revolt broke out on board the *Creole*, en route from Virginia to Louisiana with a cargo of 135 slaves. Nineteen of the blacks seized control of the vessel, killing one man and wounding several others. They sailed to Nassau, where officials set all of the slaves free. What this amounted to was the most successful slave uprising in American history, achieved because of British assistance. Some abolitionists argued that slavery existed only by virtue of state law and had no just claim to the national government's protection on the high seas. But Webster as secretary of state took the southern view that slaves were property protected by the United States Constitution. His strenuous efforts to secure compensation as a matter of international law bore fruit some years later when Britain paid approximately $110,000 to the American slaveholders.[43] "Here," said a contemporary antislavery critic, "we have the Federal Government putting forth and pledging all its powers to protect slavery—not within the United States . . . but on the high seas, and even in the harbor of a nation that does not acknowledge slavery!"[44]

Thus the United States government in its relation with other countries acted consistently and often aggressively as an agent of slaveholders. But that function was only one of several ways in which slavery affected American foreign policy. Consider, for instance, the attitude of the government toward Haiti. The black people of Saint Domingue, mostly enslaved, rose in a bloody revolt during the French Revolution. They defeated several attempts to re-establish European control and in 1804 declared themselves to be an independent nation. In the United States, their fierce struggle for freedom was viewed with far more alarm than sympathy. The Washington administration advanced large sums of money to help the Haitian planters in their resistance to the rebellion. To be sure, John Adams aligned himself with Toussaint L'Ouverture as a strategic move in the undeclared naval war with France, but his successor reversed that policy. Jefferson looked favorably upon Napoleon's effort to reconquer the colony, and in 1805 his government imposed an embargo upon trade with the new republic.[45]

Americans had good reason to be grateful to the Haitians, whose successful resistance to Napoleon's troops helped clear the way for the Louisiana Purchase in 1803. Yet the United States for nearly sixty years refused to recognize the independence of Haiti, whereas France and Britain did so much earlier. The principal reason for this sustained hostility was that southerners associated the black republic with their own most terrible fear. "Can the people of the South permit the intercourse which would result from establishing relations of any sort with Haiti?" demanded a Georgia senator in 1826. "Is the emancipated slave, his hands yet reeking in the blood of his murdered master, to be admitted into their ports, to spread the doctrines of insurrection, and to strengthen and invigorate them, by exhibiting in his own person an example of successful revolt?" A Missouri senator at about the same time declared that the safety of the slaveholding states would not permit "black Consuls and Ambassadors to establish themselves in our cities, and to parade through our country, and give their fellow blacks in the United States, proof in hand of the honors which await them, for a like successful effort on their part."[46] Those who advocated recognition of Haiti, said a South Carolina congressman in 1838, were "traitors—traitors not to their country only, but to the whole human race."[47] Antislavery voices responded that in refusing recognition, Americans were shamefully betraying their own principles.[48] But the southern view prevailed until the presidency of Abraham Lincoln, when diplomatic relations were at last established between the two oldest republics in the western hemisphere.

Much more difficult to assess is the influence of slavery on territorial expansion in the antebellum decades. No one any longer accepts at face value the abolitionist view that the Texan Revolution, the annexation of Texas, the war with Mexico, and the persistent efforts to acquire Cuba were components of a slaveholders' master plan for enlarging the domain of their peculiar institution. Yet the "slave-power conspiracy" thesis did not miss the mark entirely. Expansionism, to be sure, had many sources and was a national rather than a sectional phenomenon. Nevertheless it was concentrated largely in the Democratic party, and the Democratic party of the 1840s and 1850s became increasingly subservient to the South. When northern Democrats like James Buchanan and Stephen A. Douglas voted for the annexation of Texas or advocated the acquisition of Cuba, they did so—in part, at least—to gratify southern wishes and court southern favor.

For the South, Cuba signified both danger and opportunity. The danger was that slavery might somehow be abolished or overthrown on the island, which, said a South Carolina congressman, would then become "a second Hayti to cast the shadow of its ominous gloom over our shores."[49] In response to the southern feeling, the United States government repeatedly opposed any action likely to encourage servile rebellion or promote emancipation in Cuba.[50] On the other hand, annexation of the island would strengthen southern political power within the Union and perhaps inspire further American expansion into the Caribbean and Central America. Northern as well as southern orators might justify such expansion on economic or humanitarian grounds, or as a matter of national security. But Senator Albert G. Brown of Mississippi was utterly candid when he stated: "I want Cuba, and I know that sooner or later we must have it.. . . . I want Tamaulipas, Potosi, and one or two other Mexican States; and I want them all for the same reason—for the planting or spreading of slavery."[51]

Of course nothing came of the campaign for annexation of Cuba. With one sectional crisis following another after 1846, the times were not auspicious for such a venture. Antislavery forces stood fiercely opposed to the acquisition of additional slave territory, and the South itself was divided on the question. In any case, Spain remained totally unreceptive to American talk about purchasing the island. What seems most remarkable, in view of the overwhelming odds against success, is the dedication with which three Democratic administrations pursued the dream of Cuban annexation. James K. Polk, who had already presided over a vast expansion of American sovereignty, opened the bidding for Cuba in 1848 at $100 million. Franklin Pierce's efforts were vigorous and also inept, beginning with the appointment of a hyperthyroid expansionist as minister to Spain and culminating in the notorious Ostend Manifesto. Actually a diplomatic dispatch that became public knowledge, the Manifesto called for seizure of Cuba if it could not be purchased. As for James Buchanan, he recommended the acquisition of Cuba in three of his four annual messages to Congress. There was a curiously naive cynicism in his accompanying argument that transfer of the island to the United States would do much to eliminate the international slave trade.[52]

By the 1850s, much of the slave trade to Cuba was in fact conducted under the cover of the American flag. American laws against the trade, dating from 1807, were inadequately enforced, and the United States refused to join in international agreements for improving enforcement. The sticking point was British insistence upon mutual rights of search, meaning that a suspected slave ship, whatever flag it might be flying, could be stopped and examined by the naval forces of any cooperating nation. But federal officials, remembering the War of 1812, were unwilling to accept any such abridgment of American maritime rights. By clinging tenaciously to that cherished principle, freedom of the seas, the United States government seriously hampered suppression of the African slave trade. And so, even in pursuit of an avowedly *anti*slavery purpose, American foreign policy managed to take on a *pro*slavery cast.[53]

Why did a government founded upon the principles of human liberty and supposedly exemplifying those principles to the rest of the world, act so devotedly as an agent of slavery in its conduct of foreign policy? To abolitionists, the answer seemed plain enough. The slaveholding class, they said, had dominated the federal government from its inception and had systematically installed policies aimed at fortifying slavery as a national institution. Statistics on tenure of high federal offices lent some credence to such an explanation. For instance, in the nation's first sixty years under the Constitution, southerners held the presidency about 80 percent of the time, and there was a southern secretary of state 65 percent of the time. Even those figures understate the case because they do not include the northerners with strong southern ties and sympathies who came to be called "doughfaces"—men such as Martin Van Buren and James Buchanan. On the eve of the Civil War, Alexander H. Stephens acknowledged that "with but few exceptions, the South has controlled the Government in its every important action from the beginning."[54]

Reinforcing southern political power were those racial attitudes, pervasive throughout the entire country, that placed the Negro outside the whole structure of American liberty. Thus, when Lincoln argued that slavery was incompatible with the Declaration of Independence, Douglas could reply that the Declaration had been written for white men only.[55] That was the simplest way to explain how slavery could be allowed to flourish in the heartland of liberty. Of course there were other influences besides racism at work. Men like Thomas Jefferson, John Quincy Adams, and Daniel Webster, who regarded themselves as opposed to slavery, contributed significantly to shaping the pattern of proslavery diplomacy. They often did so with important considerations in mind, such as the national interest, commercial rivalry with Britain, the property rights of American citizens, sectional accommodation, and partisan advantage. But it also appears that much of the policy-making was done routinely and incrementally, without much reflection on its broader implications and with little set purpose beyond getting the day's work done.

The paradox of liberty and slavery in early American foreign policy is just one aspect of the complex relationship between liberty and slavery in early American culture as a whole. Each reinforced and subverted the other. The legal right to own slaves was itself an excessive kind of freedom, one that southerners eventually took up arms to defend and ended by destroying. Small freedoms and sometimes the promise of manumission were part of the discipline of slavery, but every taste of freedom—every discussion and every dream of it—made the United States a less favorable environment for slaveholding. Slavery contradicted the fundamental principles of the Republic and became in time a mortal threat to the constitutional structure of American freedom. Yet the names Washington, Jefferson, and Madison are eloquent reminders of the extent to which the foundations of American liberty were laid by slaveholders. And we need only think of the women's rights movement or the Fourteenth Amendment to remind ourselves of how much modern Ameri-

can liberties are derived from the struggle against slavery. It is a web of impli-
cation that grows more complicated and mysterious as one studies it.

There is a reminder of the interplay between liberty and slavery at the very
top of the Capitol in Washington. Fittingly, the statue of Freedom was lifted to
its place above the great dome in 1863, the year of the Emancipation Proclamation and of the address at Gettysburg proclaiming a "new birth of freedom."
As originally designed during the mid-1850s by sculptor Thomas Crawford,
the figure wore a freedom cap in the tradition of the French Revolution. But the
work of enlarging the Capitol was then in charge of a southerner, the secretary
of war, who objected to the freedom cap because, he said, it had originated in
ancient Rome as the emblem of a freed slave. Crawford obligingly altered
his design, and so today one sees Freedom wearing instead a feathered helmet
that was fashioned as a concession to the slaveholding sensitivities of Jefferson Davis.[56]

Stanford University

NOTES

1. William Wirt, *Sketches of the Life and Character of Patrick Henry* (15th edition,
New York, 1860), 137-142.

2. John C. Fitzpatrick, ed., *The Writings of George Washington* (39 vols., Washington,
D.C., 1931-1944), 3: 224, 242. See also p. 292.

3. On this subject, see William J. Cooper, Jr., *Liberty and Slavery: Southern Politics to
1860* (New York, 1983), 30-32.

4. M. I. Finley, "Slavery," *International Encyclopedia of the Social Sciences* (17 vols.,
New York, 1968), 14: 308; Orlando Patterson, *Slavery and Social Death* (Cambridge,
Mass., 1982), 98, 340.

5. Edmund S. Morgan, "Slavery and Freedom: The American Paradox," *Journal of
American History*, 59 (1972-1973): 5-29; Morgan, *American Slavery, American Freedom: The Ordeal of Colonial Virginia* (New York, 1975), 338-387.

6. Joel Barlow, *An Oration Delivered at the North Church in Hartford, at the Meeting
of the Connecticut Society of the Cincinnati, July 4, 1787* (Hartford, 1787), 20.

7. George Bancroft, *Literary and Historical Miscellanies* (New York, 1855), 516.

8. [Thomas Paine], *Common Sense* (Philadelphia, 1776), 58.

9. Horst Dippel, *Germany and the American Revolution, 1770-1800*, translated by
Bernhard A. Uhlendorf (Chapel Hill, N.C., 1977), 149, 151.

10. Philip S. Foner, *The Democratic-Republican Societies, 1790-1800: A Documentary
Sourcebook of Constitutions, Declarations, Addresses, Resolutions, and Toasts* (West-
port, Conn., 1976), 353.

11. Jefferson to William Short, 3 January 1793, in Andrew A. Lipscomb, ed., *The Writings of Thomas Jefferson* (20 vols., Washington, D.C., 1903-1904), 9: 9-13.

12. *Annals of Congress*, 15 Cong., 1 sess., 1482.

13. William R. Manning, ed., *Diplomatic Correspondence of the United States Concerning the Independence of the Latin-American Nations* (3 vols., New York, 1925), 1: 146; Charles Carroll Griffin, *The United States and the Disruption of the Spanish Empire, 1810-1822* (New York, 1937), 121-160, 244-276; Harry Ammon, *James Monroe: The Quest for National Identity* (New York, 1971), 409-448; Samuel Flagg Bemis, *John Quincy Adams and the Foundations of American Foreign Policy* (New York, 1949), 341-362.

14. Manning, ed., *Diplomatic Correspondence*, 193.

15. Dated 25 May 1821, the appeal was first published in the *North American Review*, 17 (1823): 414-416.

16. Charles Francis Adams, ed., *Memoirs of John Quincy Adams, Comprising Portions of His Diary from 1795 to 1848* (12 vols., Philadelphia, 1874-1877), 6: 173, 198-199; *Annals of Congress*, 18 Cong., 1 sess., 1085-1099, 1170-1177. Myrtle A. Cline, *American Attitude toward the Greek War of Independence, 1821-1828* (Atlanta, Ga., 1930), 151, 158, 168-174; Harris J. Booras, *Hellenic Independence and America's Contribution to the Cause* (Rutland, Vt., 1934), 183-192, 212-215.

17. James D. Richardson, ed., *A Compilation of the Messages and Papers of the Presidents* (10 vols., Washington, D.C., 1896-1899), 2: 193, 217, 259-260; Cline, *American Attitude*, 199-200, 203-204.

18. Richardson, *Messages and Papers*, 2: 501.

19. Merli Curti, "Austria and the United States, 1848-1852," *Smith College Studies in History*, 11 (1925-1926): 150-153.

20. *The Writings and Speeches of Daniel Webster* (18 vols., Boston, 1903), 12: 171; 13: 461, 462. The letter to J. G. Hulsemann, Austrian chargé d'affaires in Washington, was written 21 December 1850; the Kossuth speech was delivered 7 January 1852.

21. *Congressional Globe*, 32 Cong., 1 sess., 104-106.

22. Ibid., 165. The congressman was Meredith P. Gentry.

23. Ibid., 28 Cong., 2 sess., App., 73. The congressman was Samuel C. Sample. See Albert K. Weinberg, *Manifest Destiny: A Study of Nationalist Expansionism in American History* (Baltimore, 1935), 100-129.

24. Lord Aberdeen to Richard Pakenham, 26 December 1843; John C. Calhoun to Pakenham, 18 April 1844, in William R. Manning, ed., *Diplomatic Correspondence of the United States: Inter-American Affairs, 1831-1860* (12 vols., Washington, 1932-39), 7: 18-22, 252-253.

25. Hunter Miller, *Treaties and Other International Acts of the United States of America*, vol. 2 (Washington, D.C., 1931): 99-100, 155.

26. Benjamin Quarles, *The Negro in the American Revolution* (Chapel Hill, N.C., 1961), 158-181.

27. Charles R. Ritcheson, *Aftermath of Revolution: British Policy Toward the United States, 1783-1795* (Dallas, 1969), 70-75, 100, 236; Donald L. Robinson, *Slavery in the Structure of American Politics, 1765-1820* (New York, 1971), 348-349; Howard Albert

Ohline, "Politics and Slavery: The Issue of Slavery in National Politics, 1787-1815," Ph.D. dissertation, University of Missouri, Columbia, 1969, pp. 265-267.

28. Frederic Austin Ogg, "Jay's Treaty and the Slavery Interests of the United States," *Annual Report of the American Historical Association for the Year 1901* (Washington, 1902), 1: 275-298; Robinson, *Slavery in American Politics*, 349-361; Arnett G. Lindsay, "Diplomatic Relations between the United States and Great Britain Bearing on the Return of Negro Slaves, 1783-1828," *Journal of Negro History*, 5 (1920): 391-408.

29. Miller, *Treaties*, 2: 574-575.

30. *American State Papers* (38 vols., Washington, D.C., 1834), *Foreign Relations*, 4: 106-126, 348-407; Miller, *Treaties*, 2: 660-661; Bemis, *Adams and American Foreign Policy*, 231-233, 293.

31. Adams, *Memoirs*, 5: 160.

32. *American State Papers, Foreign Relations*, 5: 220; 6: 351-355, 637-638; Miller, *Treaties*, 3: 91-140, 261-268; John Bassett Moore, *History and Digest of the International Arbitrations to Which the United States Has Been a Party* (6 vols., Washington, D.C., 1898), 1: 350-390; Lindsay, "Return of Negro Slaves," 409-419.

33. Julian P. Boyd, *The Papers of Thomas Jefferson* (21 vols to date, Princeton, N.J., 1950-1983), 17: 472-473n, 638-639; 19: 430-436, 518-520; Ohline, "Politics and Slavery," 187-192.

34. Jackson to Edmund P. Gaines, 8 April 1816, John Spencer Bassett, ed. *Correspondence of Andrew Jackson* (6 vols., Washington, D.C., 1927), 2: 238-239; James W. Silvver, *Edmund Pendleton Gaines, Frontier General* (Baton Rouge, La., 1949), 59-63.

35. An account of the destruction of the fort written by the American naval officer in command is Jairus Loomis to Daniel T. Patterson, 13 Aug. 1816, in *American State Papers, Foreign Relations*, 4: 559-560. An extensive secondary account is in James Parton, *Life of Andrew Jackson* (3 vols., New York, 1860), 2: 397-407.

36. Daniel T. Patterson to Benjamin W. Crowninshield, *American State Papers, Foreign Relations*, 4: 561.

37. William R. Manning, *Early Diplomatic Relations Between the United States and Mexico* (Baltimore, 1916), 229-231, 240-246, 250-251.

38. J. Fred Rippy, "Border Troubles Along the Rio Grande, 1848-1860," *Southwestern Historical Quarterly*, 23 (1919-1920): 99-104; Ronnie C. Tyler, "The Callahan Expedition of 1855: Indians or Negroes?" *Southwestern Historical Quarterly*, 70 (1966-1967): 574-585; Paul Neff Garber, *The Gadsden Treaty* (Philadelphia, 1923), 159-160.

39. William R. Manning, ed., *Diplomatic Correspondence of the United States: Canadian Relations, 1784-1860* (4 vols., Washington, 1940-1945), 1:294, 909-910. For Henry Clay's efforts, see ibid., 2: 100-101, 110, 132-133, 135, 181, 634-635, 771-772.

40. Roman J. Zorn, "Criminal Extradition Menaces the Canadian Haven for Fugitive Slaves, 1841-61," *Canadian Historical Review*, 38 (1957): 284-294; William Renwick Riddell, "The Fugitive Slave in Upper Canada," *Journal of Negro History*, 5 (1920): 342-357; Robin W. Winks, *The Blacks in Canada: A History* (New Haven, 1971), 174-175.

41. Stevenson to Lord Palmerston, 29 July 1836. Other long letters are those of 12 May 1837; 23 Dec. 1837; 4 Dec. 1838, Andrew Stevenson Papers, Manuscript Division, Library of Congress.

42. Stevenson to Secretary of State John Forsyth, 8 May, 6 Aug. 1839, Andrew Stevenson Papers, Library of Congress; Joe Bassette Wilkins, Jr., "Window on Freedom: The South's Response to the Emancipation of the Slaves in the British West Indies, 1833-1861," Ph.D. dissertation, University of South Carolina, 1977, pp. 166-197.

43. Webster to Edward Everett, 29 Jan. 1842, in Kenneth E. Shewmaker, *et al.*, eds., *The Papers of Daniel Webster: Diplomatic Papers, Volume 1, 1841-1843* (Hanover, N.H., 1983), 177-185; Wilkins: "Window on Freedom," 197-206; Howard Jones, "The Peculiar Institution and National Honor: The Case of the *Creole* Slave Revolt," *Civil War History*, 21 (1975): 28-50.

44. [William Jay], *The Creole Case and Mr. Webster's Despatch; with the Comments of the N.Y. American* (New York, 1842), 12.

45. Robinson, *Slavery in American Politics*, 361-377; Rayford W. Logan, *The Diplomatic Relations of the United States with Haiti, 1776-1891* (Chapel Hill, N.C., 1941), 32-187; Timothy Morrison Matthewson, "Slavery and Diplomacy: The United States and Saint Domingue, 1791-93," Ph.D. dissertation, University of California, Santa Barbara, 1976.

46. *Register of the Debates of Congress*, 19 Cong., 1 sess., 291, 330. The senators were John M. Berrien and Thomas Hart Benton.

47. Mary S. Legaré, ed., *Writings of Hugh Swinton Legaré, Late Attorney General and Acting Secretary of State of the United States* (2 vols., Charleston, 1846), 1: 327.

48. Washington *National Era*, 23 Dec. 1852.

49. [James Hamilton], *Speech of Mr. Hamilton, of South Carolina, on the Panama Mission, Delivered in the House of Representatives, April 6, 1826* (Washington, D.C., 1826), 24; Philip S. Foner, *A History of Cuba and Its Relations with the United States* (2 vols., New York, 1962-1963), 1: 150-169; 2: 75-85. C. Stanley Urban, "The Africanization of Cuba Scare, 1853-55," *Hispanic American Historical Review*, 37 (1957): 29-45.

50. Henry Clay to Henry Middleton, 26 Dec. 1825, and Martin Van Buren to Cornelius P. Van Ness, 2 Oct. 1829, in Manning, ed., *Diplomatic Correspondence, Independence of Latin-American Nations*, 1: 266, 306; Clay to Richard C. Anderson and John Sergeant, 8 May 1826, in *Register of the Debates of Congress*, 20 Cong., 2 sess., App., 45-46; Daniel Webster to Robert B. Campbell, 14 Jan. 1843, in Manning, ed., *Diplomatic Correspondence, Inter-American Affairs*, 11: 27.

51. Speech at Hazelhurst, Miss., 11 Sept. 1858, in M. W. Cluskey, ed., *Speeches, Messages, and Other Writings of the Hon. Albert G. Brown* (2nd ed., Philadelphia, 1859), 595.

52. Foner, *History of Cuba*, 2: 9-40; Robert E. May, *The Southern Dream of a Caribbean Empire, 1854-1861* (Baton Rouge, La., 1973), 23, 30-76, 163-189; Richard Kerwin MacMaster, "The United States, Great Britain and the Suppression of the Cuban Slave Trade, 1835-1860," Ph.D. dissertation, Georgetown University, 1968, pp. 257-295, 337-386; Frederick Shriver Klein, *President James Buchanan: A Biography* (University Park, Pa., 1962), 234-241, 324-345; Richardson, *Messages and Papers*, 5: 510-511, 561, 642.

53. W. E. B. Du Bois, *The Suppression of the African Slave Trade to the United States of America, 1638-1870* (Cambridge, Mass., 1896), 131-150. Hugh H. Soulsby, *The Right of Search and the Slave Trade in Anglo-American Relations, 1814-1862* (Baltimore, 1933); Bemis, *Adams and American Foreign Policy*, 412-415, 423-435.

54. Richard Malcolm Johnston and William Hand Browne, *Life of Alexander H. Stephens* (Philadelphia, 1883), 375.

55. Roy P. Basler, *et al.*, eds., *The Collected Works of Abraham Lincoln* (9 vols., New Brunswick, N.J., 1953-1955), 2: 499-501, 519-520; 3: 9-10, 16, 29, 79-81, 112-113, 177-178, 262-263, 296.

56. Jefferson Davis to Montgomery C. Meigs, 15 Jan. 1856, in Dunbar Rowland, ed., *Jefferson Davis, Constitutionalist: His Letters, Papers, and Speeches* (10 vols., Jackson, Miss., 1923), 10: 40-41. Robert L. Gale, *Thomas Crawford, American Sculptor* (Pittsburgh, 1964), 124, 155, 156.

Lincoln and Liberty

by James M. McPherson

On 18 April 1864 Abraham Lincoln took the train to Baltimore where he gave a short speech at the opening of the Maryland Sanitary Fair, a fund-raising event for that remarkable Civil War counterpart of the modern Red Cross and USO, the United States Sanitary Commission. Lincoln's visit to Baltimore occurred against a backdrop of three years of grueling, destructive war. It came on the eve of Union military offensives in Virginia and Georgia that were destined to be more lethal and relentless than anything that had gone before. More than a year earlier Lincoln had issued the Emancipation Proclamation, and just ten days before this Baltimore speech the Senate had passed a 13th Amendment to the Constitution to end chattel slavery forever in the United States.

"The world has never had a good definition of the word liberty, and the American people, just now, are much in want of one," said Lincoln on this occasion. "We all declare for liberty; but in using the same *word* we do not all mean the same *thing*. With some the word liberty may mean for each man to do as he pleases with himself, and the product of his labor; while with others the same may mean for some men to do as they please with other men, and the product of other men's labor. Here are two, not only different, but incompatible things, called by the same name—liberty." Lincoln went on to illustrate his point with a parable about animals. "The shepherd drives the wolf from the sheep's throat," he said, "for which the sheep thanks the shepherd as a *libera-tor*, while the wolf denounces him for the same act as the destroyer of liberty, especially as the sheep is a black one. Plainly the sheep and the wolf are not agreed upon a definition of the word liberty; and precisely the same difference prevails to-day among us human creatures, even in the North, and all professing to love liberty. Hence we behold the processes by which thousands are daily passing from under the yoke of bondage, hailed by some as the advance of liberty, and bewailed by others as the destruction of all liberty."[1]

The shepherd in this fable was, of course, Lincoln himself; the black sheep was the slave, and the wolf his owner. Lincoln chose to tell this story in a city where three years earlier a regiment of Massachusetts soldiers on their way to defend the capital had been attacked by a mob. This incident produced, among other things, one of the Confederacy's favorite poems, set to music as "Maryland, My Maryland," and written by a native of Baltimore, in which Lincoln is denounced as a "despot" and "tyrant" trying to snuff out liberty in Maryland and the South. And even as Lincoln spoke, in April 1864, Marylanders were debating a proposal to amend their own constitution to abolish slavery in the state—a proposal that split the white population down the middle, with one side supporting it as a step toward liberty, the other condemning it as a despotic blow against liberty. And of course it was almost exactly a year later that another native of Maryland assassinated Lincoln in the name of liberty, shouting as he jumped to the stage of Ford's Theater, "Sic semper tyrannis!"—Thus always to tyrants!

To us, today, it seems self-evident that the emancipation of four million slaves from bondage was a great triumph of liberty. But for a majority of white Americans in the Civil War era—until almost the end of the war—this accomplishment represented the antithesis of liberty. By a majority of white Americans I mean most southerners and more than two-fifths of the northerners—the Democrats, who opposed emancipation to the bitter end. It was the outcome of the war that transformed and expanded the concept of liberty to include abolition of slavery, and it was Lincoln who was the principal agent of this transformation.

Lincoln's complaint that the world had never had a good definition of liberty was well founded. The problem is that there are too many definitions. The *Oxford English Dictionary* has eight major definitions of liberty, with historical illustrations. One historian of ideas has recorded some two hundred definitions that run the gamut from natural liberty, civil liberties, intellectual freedom, religious liberty, to toleration of eccentricities or of deviant personal behavior, freedom of the will, and equality of voting rights in republican self-government. The foremost philosopher of liberty in Lincoln's time—perhaps of all time—was John Stuart Mill, who defined liberty as "protection against the tyranny of the political rulers," a concept that involved the limitation "of the power which can be legitimately exercised by the society over the individual."[2] The leading American political scientist of Lincoln's generation, Francis Lieber, defined liberty as "a high degree of untrammeled political action in the citizen, and an acknowledgment of his dignity and his important rights by the government."[3] A modern historian has pointed out that from the beginning Americans have "associated liberty primarily with their rejection of coercive authority," especially the authority of government.[4] The classic statement of American liberty—the Magna Charta of the United States, as it were—is the Declaration of Independence. "All men are created equal," wrote Thomas Jefferson, and "endowed by their Creator with certain unalienable rights," including "life, liberty, and the pursuit of happiness." Governments are instituted "to secure these rights," but they derive "their just powers from the consent of the governed," so that "whenever any form of government becomes destructive of these ends, it is the right of the people to alter or abolish it."

The question of *which* men were included among the "all men" whom Jefferson declared "created equal"—and indeed, whether the generic term "men" included women—would later become significant, as we shall see. For now it is sufficient to note that common to all of the foregoing definitions of liberty is the assumption that the main sphere of liberty is political, and that the greatest potential threat to the liberties and rights of the individual comes from government itself. Though government is necessary to protect a citizen's liberty, it must also be prevented from becoming so strong or corrupt as to undermine that same liberty. Most American writings about the concept of liberty over the past three centuries have focused on *civil* liberties and their relationship to government. This is scarcely surprising, for the national consciousness—indeed the nation itself—was forged in the struggle for these civil liberties against what Americans considered overweening government power. This consciousness—this struggle—also helps to explain the paradox of the coexistence of American liberty and American slavery.

Many of the Founding Fathers were preoccupied with the threat of government to liberty. They tended to see all political history, back at least as far as classical Greece and Rome, as a conflict between liberty and power, with liberty usually losing in the end to the aggrandizement of centralized power by a Caesar, a tyrant, an emperor, a king. Republics based on the liberties and equal rights of citizens under law had been fragile and usually short-lived experiments. Eternal vigilance against the aggressions of government was indeed the price of liberty. At great cost, Englishmen from the days of the Magna Charta down to the Glorious Revolution of 1688 had carved out an enlarged sphere of liberty and self-government through their representatives in Parliament, curtailing and limiting the powers of the crown in the process. It was these rights and liberties of Englishmen that Americans fought for in their revolution of 1776. It was this fragile experiment in republicanism that they sought to protect against the threat of overweening power, by adopting a bill of rights, by instituting a series of checks and balances and a division of powers within the national government, and by creating a federal system that fragmented power among national, state, and local governments.

Thus when Americans of the revolutionary and post-revolutionary generations spoke of liberty, they usually meant the rights of states and localities, the freedom of the press, of speech, of assembly, of religion, the right to security in person and home against unwarranted search and seizure, the right to bear arms, the right to a trial by jury, the sanctity of property, and the writ of habeas corpus. These were the birthrights, in principle and in practice, of Americans of European descent. A good many of the Founding Fathers might have considered them the birthright, in principle at least, of all other Americans as well. They believed that in theory the phrase "All men are created equal" meant just what it said. In a word, they believed the enslavement of Americans of African descent to be wrong, contrary to the ideals of liberty they had fought for in the Revolution.

But they were faced with a condition, not a theory; a reality, not an ideal. The reality was the existence of slavery in all of the colonies that rebelled against Britain and most of the states that ratified the Constitution, a reality rooted a century or more deep in custom, law, and economics. Wherever the economic roots were shallow and the number of slaves was not large—north of the Mason-Dixon line—the libertarian ideology of the Revolution managed to accomplish the abolition of slavery. But south of the line, liberty and slavery grew up together with a diminishing sense of their incompatibility after 1800. By the generation before the Civil War most white southerners—and a good many northerners as well—not only considered liberty and slavery quite compatible, but even believed that the slavery of blacks was essential to the liberty of whites.

One obstacle to applying the concept of liberty to slaves lay in their legal status as property. The right of property was an essential part of the American notion of liberty; as the political scientist Francis Lieber put it, "one of the staunchest principles of civil liberty is the firmest possible protection of individual property."[5] John Adams insisted that "property is surely a right of mankind as really as liberty." Even his radical cousin Sam Adams asked: "What liberty can there be, when property is taken away without consent?"[6] The 5th Amendment to the Constitution states that no person shall be deprived of "life, liberty, or property, without due process of law." Antislavery people insisted that this provision mandated the *liberty* of black people in the territories, where the national government had jurisdiction; but the Supreme Court, in the Dred Scott decision of 1857, sanctioned instead the proslavery position that this Amendment protected the slaveowner's right to take his human *property* into the territories and have it protected there. Slaves, said the Court, were not persons under the Constitution and therefore had no right to liberty. Indeed, in Chief Justice Roger Taney's words, black persons whether slave *or* free "had no rights which the white man was bound to respect."[7]

In another sense also the notion of property inhibited any application of the concept of liberty to slaves. An essential component of liberty under a republican government, as Thomas Jefferson and his followers viewed it, was *independence.* The opposite of independence, of course, was *dependence.* A man who depended on another for his living was not truly free—he was subject to the authority, to the orders and manipulation, of the man who paid his wages and who therefore dictated the terms of his existence. Independence—and therefore liberty—could be achieved only by the ownership of productive property: a farm, a business, or a trade in which the skilled artisan owned his tools and was paid directly by the purchaser for the fruits of his labor rather than paid wages for his work. Only a society of property-owning farmers, artisans, tradesmen, and professionals could sustain a republican government; the growth of a large class without property would eventually bring down republican self-government and erect a despotism in its place. That is why Jefferson feared the growth of a wage-earning propertyless class as "sores on the body politic." That is why most state constitutions initially required the ownership of property, or at least the paying of taxes, as a qualification for voting. Women were dependent; children were dependent; slaves were dependent; propertyless laborers were dependent. Therefore they were subject to the authority of their husbands, fathers, masters, or employers; that is why they were defined *out* of the body politic of freemen who owned property and enjoyed the civil and political liberty of self-government in a republic.

Of course, with the rise of industrialization and immigration after 1820, a substantial wage-earning class of white men grew up owning little if any property. Various kinds of protests and responses to this development fueled the politics and political economy of the Jacksonian era. One response was to broaden the definition of political liberty and self-government by eliminating property and tax-paying qualifications for voting in most states. One's labor power became, in effect, a form of property qualifying one for liberty—that is, if you were free, white, twenty-one, and male.

But the notion of independence as a fundamental part of liberty persisted, and became bound up with racism, especially in the South, to create an ideology of black slavery as the necessary basis of white liberty. The first part of this ideology was the "mud-sill" philosophy, expressed by many southern thinkers in th 1850s, most bluntly by Senator James Hammond of South Carolina in his famous King Cotton speech of 1858. "In all social systems there must be a class to do the menial duties, to perform the drudgery of life," said Hammond. "It constitutes the very mud-sill of society." Turning to senators from northern states, Hammond said that "your whole hireling class of manual laborers and 'operatives,' as you call them, are essentially slaves. The difference between us is, that our slaves are hired for life . . . yours are hired by the day."[8]

Hammond here reformulated the old Jeffersonian theme that liberty required independence—that is, ownership of property. Because most of the unskilled, propertyless workers in the South were black slaves, a larger proportion of southern whites than of northern whites owned actual property; but more important, they all owned the most vital property of all, a white skin. This "herrenvolk democracy"—the equality of all who belonged to the master race—became the perceived basis for white liberty in the South. It was a reading of the Declaration of Independence that said "all *white* men are created equal." As John C. Calhoun, the leading southern political leader, phrased it: "With us the two great divisions of society are not the rich and the poor, but white and black; and all the former, the poor as well as the rich, belong to the upper class, and are respected and treated as equals."[9] Alabama's fire-eating orator William Lowndes Yancey declared in 1860 that "your fathers and my fathers built this government on two ideas. The first is that the white race is the citizen, and the master race, and the white man is the equal of every other white man. The second idea is that the negro is the inferior race."[10] Therefore, echoed another Alabama political leader, "slavery secures the equality of the white race, and upon its permanent establishment rests the hope of democratic liberty." Or as one of the South's leading newspapers, the *Richmond Enquirer*, put it succinctly in 1856: "Freedom is not possible without slavery."[11]

This idea was by no means confined to the South alone. Many northern workingmen shared it—especially Irish immigrants and other wage-earners at the bottom of the social scale, where they feared competition with blacks, particularly if the slaves were freed and came north looking for jobs. This fear sparked many of the anti-Negro riots in northern cities from the 1830s to 1860s, including the largest of all, the New York draft riots of 1863. This herrenvolk theme of white supremacy was also a fundamental premise of the Democratic party, and Stephen A. Douglas was one of its principal spokesmen, most notably in his famous debates with Lincoln in 1858.

For Lincoln rejected the notion that the rights of liberty and the pursuit of happiness were confined to the white race. He was not the only American to challenge this dogma, of course. From the beginning of their movement, abolitionists had insisted that black people were equal to whites in the sight of God and equally entitled to liberty in this world. Indeed, the abolitionists and the radical wing of the Republican party went farther than Lincoln in maintaining the principle of equal rights for all people. But because of his prominence as a Republican party leader after 1858 and his power as President of the United States after 1860, Lincoln's were the opinions that mattered most and that are, of course, of most interest to us.

Lincoln had always considered slavery an institution "founded on both injustice and bad policy," as he told the Illinois legislature in 1837. But he nevertheless indulged in the American habit of describing the United States as a "free country" that enjoyed more "civil and religious liberty," more "human liberty, human right" than any other people in the history of the world. Even as late as 1861 Lincoln could refer to "the free institutions which we have unceasingly enjoyed for three-quarters of a century."[12] But a decade earlier Lincoln had begun to question just how free those institutions were, so long as slavery existed in this otherwise free country. The "monstrous injustice of slavery," he said in 1854, "deprives our republican example of its just influence in the world—enables the enemies of free institutions, with plausibility, to taunt us as

hypocrites." In the 1850s Lincoln began to insist, contrary to the belief of perhaps two-thirds of white Americans, that the Declaration of Independence was
not merely "the white-man's charter of freedom." "The negro is included in the
word 'men' used in the Declaration," he maintained. This "is the great fundamental principle upon which our free institutions rest," and "negro slavery is
violative of that principle" because the black man is "entitled to . . . the right
to life, liberty, and the pursuit of happiness. I hold that he is as much entitled to
these as the white man. I agree with Judge Douglas he is not my equal in many
respects"—here Lincoln stopped short of the abolitionist affirmation of full
equality—but, Lincoln continued, "in the right to eat the bread, without leave
of anybody else, which his own hand earns, he is my equal and the equal of
Judge Douglas, and the equal of every living man."[13]

Lincoln did not consider this a new definition of liberty. He believed that
Thomas Jefferson and the other Founders had meant to include the Negro in
the phrase "all men are created equal," even though many of the Founders
owned slaves, for they were stating a principle that they hoped would eventually become a reality. Douglas maintained that, on the contrary, Jefferson had
not meant "all men" to include blacks—nor for that matter any race except
Caucasians. "This government was made by white men, for the benefit of
white men and their posterity forever, and should never be administered by
any except white men," insisted Douglas over and over again. "The signers of
the Declaration had no reference to the negro whatever when they declared all
men to be created equal. They [meant] white men, men of European birth and
European descent and had no reference either to the negro, the savage Indians,
the Fejee, the Malay, or any other inferior and degraded race."[14]

If a national referendum could have been held on these two definitions of
liberty—Lincoln's inclusive one and Douglas's definition exclusive of all but
white men—Douglas's position would have won. But Lincoln persisted against
the odds, denouncing Douglas's argument as representing a disastrous declension from the faith of Fathers, a declension that if it went much farther would
extinguish the light of liberty in America. The Know-Nothings, for example,
were trying to deny to white immigrants the liberties of free-born Americans.
Here was the danger, warned Lincoln in 1855. Once a nation decided that its
constitutional rights applied only to some and not to all men equally, the torch
of liberty would go out. "Our progress in degeneracy appears to me to be
pretty rapid," lamented Lincoln with reference to the Know-Nothings. "As a
nation, we began by declaring that *all men are created equal.*' We now practically read it 'all men are created equal, *except negroes.*' When the Know-Nothings get control, it will read 'all men are created equal, except negroes, *and
foreigners, and catholics.* When it comes to this I should prefer emigrating to
some other country where they make no pretence of loving liberty—to Russia,
for instance, where despotism can be taken pure, without the base alloy
of hypocrisy."[15]

To dehumanize the Negro—to insist that he was not a man—would boomerang on all of us, said Lincoln on many occasions in the 1850s. "Our reliance [must be] in the *love of liberty* . . . the preservation of the spirit which prizes liberty as the heritage of all men, in all lands, every where. Destroy this spirit, and you have planted the seeds of despotism around your own doors. Familiarize yourselves with the chains of bondage, and you are preparing your own limbs to wear them. . . . He who would *be* no slave, must consent to *have* no slave. Those who deny freedom to others, deserve it not for themselves. . . . Accustomed to trample on the rights of those around you, you have lost the genius of your own independence, and become the fit subjects of the first cunning tyrant who rises." The Democratic party of 1859, said Lincoln in that year, had departed so far from the ideas of its founder Thomas Jefferson that it "hold[s] the *liberty* of one man to be absolutely nothing, when in conflict with another man's right of *property*." The only liberty that many whites seemed to believe in was "the liberty of making slaves of other people."[16]

"That is the real issue," said Lincoln in the peroration of his last debate with Douglas. "That is the issue that will continue in this country when these poor tongues of Judge Douglas and myself shall be silent. It is the eternal struggle between these two principles—right and wrong . . . from the beginning of time. . . . The one is the common right of humanity and the other the divine right of kings. . . . No matter in what shape it comes, whether from a king who seeks to bestride the people of his own nation and live by the fruit of their labor, or from one race of men as an apology for enslaving another race, it is the same tyrannical principle." To prevent this principle from "eradicating the light of liberty in this American people," Lincoln pleaded, "let us re-adopt the Declaration of Independence, and with it, the practices, and policy, which harmonize with it. . . . If we do this, we shall not only have saved the Union; but we shall have so saved it, as to make, and to keep it, forever worthy of the saving."[17]

It was Lincoln's eloquent definition—or redefinition—of liberty that the South most feared. So when he won the presidency, southern states seceded in the name of their own liberties of property and state sovereignty, in the name of their right proclaimed by the Declaration of Independence to "alter or abolish" the form of government if it became destructive of the purpose of protecting their property. Southerners, said an Alabama newspaper in 1861, were a "liberty loving people," and therefore "the same spirit of freedom and independence that impelled our Fathers to the separation from the British Government" would inspire the South's fight for independence from a tyrannical and oppressive government dominated by Black Republican Yankees. A Georgia secessionist declared that southerners would be "either *slaves in the Union or freemen out of it.*"[18] One of four brothers from Texas who enlisted in the Confederate army said that like their forefathers of 1776, he and his brothers "are now enlisted in 'The Holy Cause of Liberty and Independence.'" Another

Texan called for all true sons of the Lone Star State to rally "to the standard of Liberty and Equality for white men" against "our Abolition enemies who are pledged to prostrate the white freemen of the South down to equality with negroes."[19] And Jefferson Davis appealed to his people to "renew such sacrifices as our fathers made to the holy cause of constitutional liberty . . . [with] the high and solemn motive of defending and protecting the rights . . . which our fathers bequeathed to us" from "the tyranny of an unbridled majority, the most odious . . . form of despotism."[20]

Northern Republicans, including Lincoln, ridiculed these southern claims to be fighting for liberty. For Confederates to compare their cause to the Revolution, wrote William Cullen Bryant, the poet and editor of the *New York Evening Post*, was an atrocious libel on the men of 1776. The Founding Fathers, said Bryant, fought "to establish the rights of man . . . and principles of universal liberty." The South, by contrast, was rebelling "not in the interest of general humanity, but of a domestic despotism . . . their motto is not liberty, but slavery."[21]

Northerners could not deny the South's right of revolution for just cause. All Americans, as heirs of 1776, believed in that right. Revolution, said Lincoln in 1861, is "a moral right, when exercised for a morally justifiable cause. When exercised without such a cause revolution is no right, but simply a wicked exercise of physical power."[22] That phrase, "for a morally justifiable cause," was crucial. The South had no just cause, in Lincoln's view. The immediate cause of secession was the election of a president they did not like, by perfectly legal means under a Constitution that all Americans had sworn to obey. The long-term cause was the fear that a Republican administration would restrict and harm slavery, which southerners defined as liberty. But for Lincoln, slavery was slavery; not liberty, but its opposite. Thus secession was nothing more than "a wicked exercise of physical power."

Even before he committed himself in the second year of the Civil War to emancipation as a war aim, Lincoln repeatedly insisted that it was the North, not the South, that fought to preserve the revolutionary heritage of liberty. The republic that the Founding Fathers had established as a bulwark of liberty was a fragile, vulnerable experiment in a world populated by kings, emperors, Czars, and dictators. Most republics through history had been overthrown by counter-revolutions; the French republics created by that country's revolutions had twice succumbed to emperors and had once seen the Bourbon monarchy restored. The United States represented, in Lincoln's words, "the last, best hope" for the survival of republican liberties in the world. European conservatives regularly predicted that this upstart democracy would collapse; a successful rebellion by the South would confirm that prediction. "The central idea of this struggle," said Lincoln in 1861, "is the necessity of proving that popular government is not an absurdity. We must settle this question now, whether in a free government the minority have the right to break up the government whenever they choose." The struggle, moreover, was "not altogether for today," Lincoln maintained. "It is for a vast future." It "embraces more than the fate of these United States. It presents to the whole family of man the question whether a constitutional republic, a democracy," a nation "conceived in Liberty, and dedicated to the proposition that all men are created equal," as Lincoln expressed it in the Gettysburg Address, "can long endure."[23]

Slavery was not the only problem that involved the question of liberty during the Civil War. In any war the civil liberties of citizens are liable to become victims of the passions or necessities of the conflict. During World War I hundreds of German-Americans, pacifists, and radicals went to jail and tens of thousands of others lost their freedom of speech, press, assembly, and other civil liberties. In the first months of American participation in World War II, the government rounded up and interned more than one hundred thousand Americans whose only crime was their Japanese ancestry. These violations of civil liberties occurred in wars fought far from American shores. The Civil War posed an even greater potential threat to civil liberties. By its very nature a civil war produces a more intense concern with internal security than a foreign war. Martial law prevails over large parts of a country wracked by civil war; newspapers and other media of communication are often muzzled; enemy partisans and sympathizers are arbitrarily arrested and jailed, sometimes tortured and murdered.

Both sides in the American Civil War experienced an erosion of civil liberties during the conflict. One of Lincoln's first wartime orders as commander in chief was to suspend the privilege of the writ of habeas corpus in portions of Maryland wracked by guerrilla activities and mob attacks on Union forces. If the Confederates gained control of Maryland by such actions, the national capital would be surrounded by enemy territory and the North would lose the war before it had fairly started. Northern soldiers arrested numerous pro-southern citizens in Maryland, including the mayor and police chief of Baltimore and thirty-one members of the state legislature, and clapped them in prison for months and in a few cases for more than a year without trial. Lincoln eventually extended the suspension of the writ of habeas corpus to the whole country in cases of what he defined as "disloyal persons [who] are not adequately restrained by the ordinary processes of law from . . . giving aid and comfort in various ways to the insurrection."[24] By the time the war was over, Union soldiers had arrested and detained in prison without charge at least fifteen thousand civilians, while military courts had tried and convicted hundreds of others.

Most of those arrests took place in the border slave states of Maryland, Kentucky, and Missouri where loyalties were divided and active fighting was going on, or in portions of Confederate states occupied by conquering Union forces. Most of those arrested had in fact engaged in activities with military significance, such as guerrilla attacks on Union soldiers, burning of bridges, blowing up of supply dumps, and the like. But some men were arrested for merely speaking or writing in favor of peace with the Confederacy or against the war policies of the Union government, and some of those arrested lived in northern states far from active war zones. One of the most notorious wartime violations of civil liberties occurred in Ohio where a military court convicted Democratic gubernatorial candidate Clement Vallandigham of treason for speaking out against the war. Lincoln commuted the sentence from imprisonment to banishment, and Vallandigham went to Canada, from where he conducted his unsuccessful campaign for governor of Ohio. Another celebrated case concerned one Lambdin P. Milligan, a civilian resident of Indiana who was convicted of treason by a military court in 1864 for aiding Confederate agents trying to foment an uprising in the North. After the war the Supreme Court overturned Milligan's conviction in a ruling that civilians cannot be tried by military courts in a region where the regularly established courts of the land are functioning, as they were in Indiana. Constitutional historians regard the Milligan decision as a landmark in the defense of civil liberties; some of them also interpret it as a rebuke to the Lincoln administration's record on this issue.

There was no shortage of such rebukes during the Civil War itself. In fact, northern Democrats made this issue the central theme in their attacks on Lincoln as a despot, a tyrant bent on snuffing out the liberties of white men in a calamitous and unconstitutional crusade to liberate black slaves. Countless Democratic speeches and editorials, especially at the time of Vallandigham's arrest, condemned Lincoln for suppressing "the right of the people to assemble and discuss the affairs of government, the liberty of speech and of the press, the right of trial by jury," for violating "the rights of the States and the liberties of the citizen," for "establishing a despotism." Was the government, asked a group of New York Democrats in 1863, trying to suppress rebellion in the South or "to destroy free institutions in the North"?[25] A Democratic pamphlet published in 1863 portrayed Lincoln as standing trial before the Founding Fathers, with George Washington as the prosecuting attorney. The Fathers pronounced Lincoln guilty. "You were born in the freest country under the sun," they tell the sixteenth president, "but you have converted it into a despotism. [We] now leave you, with the brand of TYRANT upon your brow."[26]

Is this how we, too, should leave Lincoln? Perhaps we should first let him speak in his own defense. Hear him on the suspension of the writ of habeas corpus, for example. By protecting individuals from arbitrary arrest and imprisonment without indictment and trial, this writ has been the safeguard of Anglo-American civil liberties for centuries. The United States Constitution specifies that the writ of habeas corpus "shall not be suspended, except when in cases of rebellion or invasion the public safety may require it." But this rebellion, said Lincoln in 1861, was precisely the kind of exceptional crisis the framers had in mind. Chief Justice Taney—author of the Dred Scott decision—

insisted that only Congress, and not the president acting in executive capacity, had the power to suspend the writ. Lincoln disagreed, and many constitutional scholars then and since have supported his position. Suspension of the writ was an emergency power; only the executive could act quickly enough in a crisis, especially if Congress was not in session. The very life of the nation was at stake, Lincoln maintained. The survival of that nation "conceived in liberty and dedicated to the proposition that all men are created equal," was the central purpose of the war. If the nation died, so did the fragile experiment in republican liberty launched in 1776. Thus the temporary suspension of habeas corpus, said Lincoln in his first message to Congress on 4 July 1861, was a small price to pay for the preservation of that larger framework of liberty, the nation itself. "Are all the laws but one [habeas corpus] to go unexecuted," asked Lincoln rhetorically, "and the government itself go to pieces, lest that one be violated?" Or as he later phrased the issue, using a simple metaphor as he often did with great effect: "By general law life *and* limb must be protected; yet often a limb must be amputated to save a life; but a life is never wisely given to save a limb. I felt that measures, otherwise unconstitutional, might become lawful, by becoming indispensable to the preservation of the constitution, through the preservation of the nation." Using another medical metaphor, Lincoln sought to allay fears that the emergency suspension of certain civil liberties during wartime would create precedents fatal to liberty in peacetime: he could no more believe that this would happen, he said, than he could "believe that a man could contract so strong an appetite for emetics during temporary illness, as to persist in feeding upon them through the remainder of his healthful life."[27]

In any event, said Lincoln, eighty percent or more of the military arrests and imprisonments of civilians were for military crimes such as sabotage, espionage, and guerrilla bushwhacking. "Under cover of 'liberty of speech,' 'liberty of the press,' and 'Habeas corpus,' " he continued, the rebels "hoped to keep on foot amongst us a most efficient corps of spies, informers, suppliers, and aiders and abettors of their cause." As for the few conspicuous cases of arrests of politicans like Vallandigham or of newspaper editors for speaking out against the war or the draft, Lincoln argued that their speeches and editorials discouraged enlistment in the army or encouraged desertions from it, thereby "damaging the army, upon the existence and vigor of which the life of the nation depends." In a rhetorical question that became one of the most famous of Lincoln's utterances, he asked: "Must I shoot a simpleminded soldier boy who deserts, while I must not touch a hair of a wily agitator who induces him to desert? . . . I think that in such a case to silence the agitator and save the boy is not only constitutional, but withal a great mercy."[28]

Such arguments did little to assuage Lincoln's critics or persuade his opponents. They saw his record on civil liberties as only part of a larger pattern of threats to traditional American liberties. Two other parts of the pattern were conscription and emancipation. Conscription, they said, robbed the citizen of a choice whether or not to serve in the army; emancipation took away the citizen's property without due process of law.

How do we, as students of history, respond to this indictment? Where do we come down on the question of Lincoln and Liberty? Do we agree with Lincoln himself that preservation of the republic created in 1776 was essential to the survival of liberty, and that all else was a necessary means to this end even if the means included a temporary suspension of some civil liberties? Do we point out that no society in the last three hundred years has been able to fight a major war without some kind of conscription, that the draft in the Civil War raised directly only ten to fifteen percent of the soldiers in the Union army, the rest of whom were volunteers, and that with its many loopholes the draft fell more lightly on the northern people than on any other people at war in modern times? Do we also point out that compared with the harrassment and imprisonment of dissidents during World War I or the internment of Japanese-Americans in World War II, the Lincoln administration's violation of civil liberties during the much greater crisis of the Civil War seems quite mild indeed? And as for emancipation—are we today more likely to identify with those four million black sheep liberated by Lincoln or with the loss of liberty by four hundred thousand wolves to prey on those sheep?

But there is a larger question involved here—nothing less than a transformation in the concept of liberty itself. To illustrate this point, I shall borrow and modify slightly the definitions worked out by the British philosopher Isaiah Berlin in a famous essay, "Two Concepts of Liberty."[29] The two concepts are Negative Liberty and Positive Liberty. The idea of negative liberty is more familiar and easier to understand. It can be defined as the absence of restraint, the freedom from interference by outside authority with our thoughts or behavior. A law requiring motorcyclists to wear a helmet would be, under this definition, to prevent them from enjoying the freedom to go bareheaded if they wish. Negative liberty, therefore, can best be understood as freedom *from.* Positive liberty is freedom *to.* This is not necessarily incompatible with negative liberty, but it has a different focus, a different emphasis. Take another example, drawn from the idea of freedom of the press. This is usually understood as a negative liberty—freedom from interference by outside authority with what a writer writes or a reader reads. But suppose I were illiterate. I would be unable to enjoy the freedom to write or read whatever I pleased, not because some authority forbade me to do so, but because I could not read or write anything. I would suffer not the absence of a negative liberty—freedom *from*—but of a positive liberty—freedom *to* read and write. The remedy would lie not in removal of restraint but in achievement of the capacity to read and write.

Another way of defining the distinction between these two concepts of liberty is to describe their relationship to power. Negative liberty and power are at opposite poles; power is the enemy of liberty, especially power concentrated in the hands of a central government. That is the kind of power that many of the Founding Fathers feared most; that is why they fragmented power in the Constitution and the federal system; that is why they wrote a bill of rights to restrain the power of the national government to interfere with individual liberty. The Bill of Rights is an excellent example of negative liberty. Nearly all of the first ten amendments to the Constitution apply the phrase "shall not" to the federal government. In fact, eleven of the first twelve amendments placed limitations on the power of the national government. But beginning with the 13th Amendment in 1865—the Amendment that abolished slavery—six of the next seven amendments radically expanded the power of the federal government at the expense of the states. The very language of these amendments illustrates the point: instead of applying the phrase "shall not" to the national government, every one of them grants significant new powers to the government with the phrase that "Congress *shall have* the power to enforce this article."

Not all of these six amendments necessarily enlarged the sphere of liberty. The 16th, for example, authorized a federal income tax, and the 18th prohibited the manufacture and sale of alcoholic beverages. But the other four amendments do offer examples of positive liberty, and they nicely illustrate the relationship between positive liberty and power. Power in these cases expanded liberty instead of repressing it; power and liberty were allies, not enemies. The emphasis was not on freedom from, but freedom to. These four amendments represent a positive expansion of liberty in another respect as well. They define *into* the population enjoying certain rights, privileges, and liberties large groups that had previously been defined *out*: black people and women. The 13th, 14th, and 15th Amendments freed the slaves and granted blacks equal civil and political rights; the 19th granted women equal political rights.

Abraham Lincoln played a crucial role in this historic shift of emphasis from negative to positive liberty. Those southerners who seceded from the Union in the name of preserving their liberties and rights—including the right to own slaves—and those northerners who denounced the Lincoln administration for violating their civil liberties, were acting in the tradition of negative liberty. Let us return to Lincoln's parable of the shepherd, the wolf, and the sheep that I quoted at the beginning of this essay. "The shepherd drives the wolf from the sheep's throat, for which the sheep thanks the shepherd as a *liberator.*" Here is Lincoln the shepherd using the great power of government and the army to achieve a positive liberty for the sheep. But the wolf was a believer in negative liberty, for to him the shepherd was "the destroyer of liberty, especially as the sheep was a black one."

Positive liberty is an open-ended concept. It has the capacity to expand toward notions of equity, justice, social welfare, equality of opportunity. For how much liberty does a starving person enjoy, except the liberty to starve? How much freedom of the press can exist in a society of illiterate people? How free is a motorcyclist who is paralyzed for life by a head injury that might have been prevented if he had worn a helmet? With the "new birth" of freedom proclaimed in the Gettysburg Address and backed by a powerful army, Lincoln helped to move the nation toward an expanded and open-ended concept of positive liberty. "On the side of the Union," he said on another occasion, this Civil War "is a struggle for maintaining in the world, that form, and substance of government, whose leading object is, to elevate the condition of men—to lift artificial weights from all shoulders—to clear the paths of laudable pursuit of all"—black as well as white—"to afford all, an unfettered start, and a fair chance, in the race of life." In "giving freedom to the slave," he declared, "we *assure* freedom to the *free*."[30]

Princeton University

NOTES

1. Roy P. Basler, ed., *The Collected Works of Abraham Lincoln*, 9 vols. (New Brunswick, N.J., 1953), 7: 301-302. Hereinafter cited as *CWL*.

2. John Stuart Mill, *On Liberty* (Harvard Classics ed.), 203, 210.

3. Francis Lieber, *On Civil Liberty and Self-Government* (Philadelphia, 1859), 37.

4. Don E. Fehrenbacher, "Introduction" to David M. Potter, *Freedom and Its Limitations in American Life* (Stanford, 1976), x.

5. Lieber, *On Civil Liberty*, 103.

6. Both Adamses quoted in Francis William Coker, ed., *Democracy, Liberty, and Property: Readings in the American Political Tradition* (New York, 1942), 125, 320.

7. The question of Negro citizenship occupies pp. 403-427 of Taney's opinion in Dred Scott v. Sandford, 19 Howard 393.

8. Selections from the *Letters and Speeches of the Hon. James H. Hammond, of South Carolina* (New York, 1866), 317-319.

9. Richard K. Crallé, ed., *The Works of John C. Calhoun*, 6 vols. (New York, 1854-1857), 4: 505-506.

10. Quoted in George M. Fredrickson, *The Black Image in the White Mind* (New York, 1971), 61.

11. Quoted in J. Mills Thornton III, *Politics and Power in a Slave Society: Alabama, 1800-1860* (Baton Rouge, 1978), 321; and James Oakes, *The Ruling Race: A History of American Slaveholders* (New York, 1982), 141.

12. *CWL*, 1: 108, 278; 2: 126; 4: 198.

13. *CWL*, 2: 255, 130; 3: 327, 16.

14. *CWL*, 3: 177, 113.

15. *CWL*, 2: 323.

16. *CWL*, 3: 95, 376, 375; 2: 250.

17. *CWL*, 3: 315, 29; 2: 276.

18. Alabama newspaper quoted in Oakes, *The Ruling Race*, 240; Georgia secessionist quoted in Michael P. Johnson, *Toward a Patriarchal Republic: The Secession of Georgia* (Baton Rouge, 1977), 36.

19. Henry Orr to Mary Orr, 31 Oct. 1861, in John Q. Anderson, ed., *Campaigning with Parsons' Texas Cavalry Brigade, CSA* (Hillsboro, Tex., 1967), 10; *LINCOLN ELECTED!* Broadside from Bell County, Texas, 8 Nov. 1860, McLelland Lincoln Collection, John Hay Library, Brown University.

20. Dunbar Rowland, ed. *Jefferson Davis, Constitutionalist: His Letters, Papers, and Speeches*, 10 vols. (Jackson, Miss., 1923), 5: 43, 202.

21. *New York Evening Post*, 18 Feb. 1861.

22. *CWL*, 4: 434n.

23. Tyler Dennett, ed., *Lincoln and the Civil War in the Diaries and Letters of John Hay* (New York, 1939), 19; *CWL*, 5: 53; 4: 422; 7: 23.

24. *CWL*, 5: 436-437.

25. Frank Freidel, ed. *Union Pamphlets of the Civil War* (Cambridge, Mass., 1967), 740-743.

26. Quoted in Don E. Fehrenbacher, "The Paradoxes of Freedom," in Fehrenbacher, *Lincoln in Text and Context: Collected Essays* (Stanford, 1987), 135.

27. *CWL*, 4: 430; 7: 281; 6: 267.

28. *CWL*, 6: 262, 266-267.

29. In Isaiah Berlin, *Four Essays on Liberty* (New York, 1970), 118-172.

30. *CWL*, 4: 438; 5: 537.

Economic Liberty and the Constitution

by Harry N. Scheiber

The phrase "economic liberty" does not appear in the United States Constitution or in the amendments, and yet few would deny that it belongs in the galaxy of what we term our constitutional values and ideals. It is similar in this regard to the "privacy" and "individual dignity" concepts which are not mentioned either in the original 1787 document or the amendments. Both logic and intuition compel one, I think, to grant the propriety of placing economic liberty alongside these other important values as implicit in the scheme of constitutional ideals and mandates that have been regarded as basic in our law.

How the concept of economic liberty connects with the explicit terms of the Constitution, how changes have appeared—in popular and jurisprudential discourse—in the concept of economic liberty over the course of two centuries' experience under the Constitution, and what bearing this history may have upon modern law and policy are the concerns of this paper.

Property and Liberty

Any search for the conceptual underpinnings of economic liberty in the Constitution's specific language leads first, of course, to the linkage with rights of property. Neither in the original document nor in the Bill of Rights—nor, for that matter, in the jurisprudence of the early Republic generally, especially the landmark decisions of the Marshall court era—do we lack in any way for evidence of the centrality of property rights to what was seen as the Constitution's basic purposes and scheme of fundamental values. Securing the "blessings of liberty" and providing for the "general welfare"—the great objectives of the new government, set forth in the Preamble—surely embraced a concern in some vital sense for the security of private rights in property. (Not an exclusive concern, nor one that negates other concerns for liberty and welfare, as some recent commentators have tried to argue, but a concern that while not unlimited or exclusive was of crucial importance.[1]) The contract clause of Article I, Sec. 10 provided a major safeguard for the security of vested property rights; the Fifth Amendment mandated that private property should not "be taken for public use, without just compensation"; and the rights of private property were further fastened into the very core of the Bill of Rights, in the classic phrasing of the Fifth Amendment's more general requirement that property (along with life and liberty) should not be taken "without due process of law."[2]

It would make analysis much simpler, to be sure, to equate economic liberty with the guarantees of security for rights of property—the constitutional doctrines that complement or are proxies for the common-law guarantees of the right to quiet possession of one's own holdings. But surely this is not nearly broad enough to comprehend the original understanding (or the various original understandings) of economic liberty as a desideratum in a free society nor as an element in the basic law. The very multiplicity of meanings given to property in the formal language of eighteenth-century political writings suggests how careful we must be to recognize multiple possible meanings for economic liberty as well.[3] Moreover, even the most dogmatic property-minded thinkers recognized that property was a bundle of rights *and obligations*, subject to regulations, taxation, and even physical taking by the power of eminent domain or emergency seizure. The long-standard interpretation portrayed the American legal environment from 1787 at least until the mid-1930s as having made the rights of property "the basic doctrine of American constitutional law"[4] so that (it was contended) until the New Deal period "the role of American law vis-a-vis private property was largely to secure it from encroachment by others. . . . [T]he owner was left with virtually uncontrolled dominion over the use and disposition of [his or her] property."[5] The "liberty" of private owners in use of their property far outweighed any formally recognized "duties" or "public obligations" attached to property ownership, it was argued, though still the obligations were always retained in form if not substance in legal and constitutional doctrine.[6]

Hence in the following overview and brief analysis of American property law in relation to economic liberty, we need to probe the purposes and the broad doctrinal implications of the public duties and obligations to which the law gave room, as well as the defenses of ownership rights that bespoke economic individualism. The dynamic of historic change in American property law is analogous to erosion by wind effects and water damage over many years; lightning seldom has struck in this segment of the landscape of legal history. Changes in the substantive content of property law have resulted largely from subtle, incremental processes of doctrinal innovation. Moreover, throughout most of the nineteenth century and much of the modern era, each state has enjoyed wide-ranging autonomy in establishing rules of property. That is, federalism as a working system has reinforced the tendency toward a diversity of rules and toward diverse patterns of change in property relationships and priorities as ordered by law.[7] By contrast, the concept of economic liberty—which has been linked closely to property rights as one conceptual underpinning in the matrix of constitutional law—has in fact undergone some dramatic moments of historic change. Two of these changes—the adoption in 1868 of the Fourteenth Amendment, and the introduction of the "preferred freedoms" doctrine by the Supreme Court in the 1930s—are critical to the discussion that follows.

Economic individualism and the common interest

The doctrines of American property law have variously served privatism, or individualistic control by owners over their holdings; or, alternatively, and in tension with the first, they have served communal or societal values and interests. Thus any linkage of "economic liberty" to property rules ought to take account of the intriguing possibility that economic liberty as a constitutional ideal may have two quite different basic meanings. The first, which is very familiar, would link the concept of liberty to the rights of the private owner to either quiet enjoyment or active use of property holdings in the marketplace. (Whether protecting the passive or a dynamic use of property, the rights in this instance are consistent with the precepts of economic individualism: these rights mark out the boundaries of a Lockean preserve within which the owner enjoys freedom from interference.) The second possible linkage of economic liberty to property, however, is one that derives from the communal and societal values that *qualify* private claims to rights in property. Its core concerns are with community interest—with a broader commitment of the law to economic liberty that embraces the whole of the citizenry and its interest in the prosperity of the larger society, not only the narrower liberty of private owners and their individualistic objectives.

We need not dwell long on the individualistic face of the law in American experience, for it is so well known. Consider for a moment, however, the record from 1790 to the Civil War. The logic of a capitalistic system makes indispensable a system of rules that give owners of private property some basis of firm reliance that will offer protection and stability: the rules of the Anglo-American common law thus traditionally afforded landed property owners valuable remedies against invasion of damage by others as well as some significant protection against government action; and both the Contract Clause and the common-law decisions of American state courts in the nineteenth century reinforced these guarantees in many ways.[8] Exemplary of the doctrines elaborated by American courts in defense of property rights was the language of Justice Patterson in the 1795 case of Van Horne's Lessee. He stated:

> The preservation of property . . . is a primary object of the social com-
> pact. . . . The rights of acquiring and possessing property and having it
> protected is one of the natural, inherent, and inalienable rights of man.[9]

A noteworthy element of this statement is the impression of dynamic, aggressive use of property and assertion of rights that Justice Patterson conveys—
speaking of "acquiring" and not only "possessing." This is a theme to which we
will return shortly. The central premise, however, that security of rights in
property was fundamental to liberty, was so consistently reiterated in the jurisprudence of the early nineteenth century that theories of republicanism can
hardly proceed without reference to it at the threshold.[10]

Of equal interest to us in thinking about property and liberty, however, is
the fact that Justice Patterson set immediately alongside his classic language on
the sacred rights of property a candid acknowledgment that public obligations
and the common weal must also have full play. He referred to the eminent
domain power, therefore, as a "despotic power . . . of taking private property
when state necessity requires"; it was a power, he continued, that "exists in
every government. . . . [G]overnment could not subsist without it."[11]

If even the most conservative formulations of jurists such as Patterson,
Chancellor James Kent, and Justice Joseph Story all recognized fully the state's
power to take property for public use under eminent domain, they also left
ample room for state action that trenched on private rights when it was necessary to use the police power for the protection and advancement of the health,
welfare, and safety of the community. The language of judicial decisions validating both police regulations and eminent-domain takings commonly referred to the public welfare and "rights of the public" (Chief Justice Taney's
phrase in his opinion in the Charles River Bridge Case), contending that when
the interests of the community were at stake private rights (whether vested or
dynamic) must yield and societal values be given priority. Among those societal values, cited regularly by the courts, were economic advancement and
prosperity of the community; it is not too much to call these goals, so mobilized as validating principles for exercises of state authority, a variant of "economic liberty" defined as the whole community's.[12]

When courts spoke of "rights of the public," they meant not only the community's right to be protected against harm from the external effects of private
uses of property—that is, the sort of protection the common law of nuisance
had long provided. The courts also invoked public rights in a positive way; the
doctrine was meant to open the channels of the law for the active protection of
a communal value, the prosperity of the community as a whole.[13]

Thus, even in the courts that provided much of the most conservative doctrine protective of vested property rights, judges such as Kent were willing to
construe liberally the powers of municipal corporations in meeting the impera-

tives of "the growing wants and prosperity" of commerce and urban life.[14] The goal of fostering rapid economic development was consistently cited in eminent domain cases to warrant takings as being "public" in their purpose and use, just as Taney had invoked "the comforts, convenience and prosperity of the people" and the community's "happiness and prosperity" in maintaining that Massachusetts could severely trench on the established rights of the Charles River Bridge proprietors.[15]

Further evidence of concern for what can fairly, I think, be termed considerations of economic liberty in community terms was found in decisions that recognized public rights in the great inland river fishery resources that so many depended upon, in those days, for food. These fisheries were said to be "a source of profit and support to multitudes of people," and so the power of property owners to act adversely to the public interest in such fisheries, even the power of the state itself to bargain away the public interest in them, was challenged and curbed by the courts.[16] Similarly, the right of citizens to take seaweed (which was used for fertilizer) from tidewaters was a right protected by courts under an ancient common-law doctrine that held such waters "strictly public" and not under control of shoreline landowners.[17] Access to the "great ponds" of New England and other such vital public resources was also given strong protection by the courts, as economic liberty diffused through the society and in the interests of community welfare and prosperity again surfaced as a determinative consideration in stating the limitations and boundaries of property owners' private rights.[18]

All these doctrinal developments—perpetuating many ancient legal rules and adapting others in a new constitutional and common-law jurisprudence designed to foster development and protect public (community) rights and interests—went forward, of course, side by side with extensive interventions in the economy by state government, augmented to some extent by federal interventions. They took the form of outright enterprise, subsidy, and grants of immunity and privilege, in order to provide the economy with the infrastructural investments in canal and (later) rail transportation that were vital in that era; to support the growth of banking institutions and capitalization; and, more generally, to support the processes of growth and development.[19] These initiatives encountered some resistance from advocates of minimalism in relation to government, though not to any very great degree until the late 1830s and after; but generally, until then at least, active government—the positive state—was viewed as propping up the foundations of economic liberty rather than as a threat to it. To the degree that there was principled opposition, it tended to focus upon issues of federalism and opposition to centralization of power rather than upon questions of "vested rights" and the claims of property against active government.[20]

Withal, the tension was seen throughout the early nineteenth century, in a variety of ways, pitting concepts of public rights and community prosperity

against the concepts of Lockean individualism and its atomistic concept of
legitimate property rights held against governmental or competitive invasion.
I think the contemporary view of economic liberty and its constitutional foundations was as much a concept bounded by communal interests and "the imperatives of progress" as it was a Lockean one bounded only by the outlines of
private property holdings and claims.[21]

On "pursuit" of happiness and the multiple definitions of "property"

The Constitution's purposes, stated in the Preamble, include securing of "the
blessings of liberty" as well as advancement of "the general welfare." The latter
is better known in constitutional lore, because the general welfare clause had
so dramatic a place in the confrontations that occurred during ratification, in
the heyday of Marshall Court nationalism, and when the high court in the
1930s abandoned older doctrines to cast the mantle of legitimacy around the
great legislative initiatives of the New Deal.[22] But the blessings-of-liberty concept also deserves a word here, for it seems to me an element of constitutional
writ with important bearing on the idea of economic liberty.

Many of the early state constitutions contained explicit provisions embodying a fusion of communal welfare ideals with privatistic values: these were the
provisions referring to *acquisition* of property (not merely ownership, or its
protection) as one of the rights associated with "the pursuit of happinesss." By
extension, one can reasonably say, these provisions were also addressed to
what contemporaries regarded as central to "the blessings of liberty." Thus the
Pennsylvania constitution declared,

> that all men are born equally free and independent, and have certain nat-
> ural, inherent, and inalienable rights, amongst which are, the enjoying
> and defending of life and liberty, acquiring, possessing and protecting
> property, and pursuing and obtaining happiness and safety.[23]

Other provisions of the same Pennsylvania document bespoke a positive conception of economic liberty for all members of the community—a conception
that vastly transcended mere concern with the security of individual owners'
vested rights. Among its guarantees were the right of persons to "emigrate
from one state or another that will receive them, or to form a new state in
vacant countries"; it also reserved to "the inhabitants of this state . . . [the]
liberty to fowl and hunt in seasonable times on . . . lands . . . not inclosed;
and in like manner to fish in all boatable waters, and others not private property."[24] Similarly, New Hampshire's first constitution provided that "acquiring,
possessing and protecting property—and in a word, . . . seeking and obtaining happiness" were among the fundamental and inherent rights of all men.[25]

The provisions of Maryland's state constitution and others that condemned monopoly or privileges bestowed by the state that were "odious, contrary to the spirit of a free government" similarly gave expression to a juridical foundation of another kind of economic liberty of the citizens.[26] Earlier, the Virginia Declaration of Rights had identified as inalienable and inherent rights the "enjoyment of life, liberty, with the means of acquiring and possessing property, and pursuing and obtaining happiness and safety"[27]—by no means a defensive concept that was meant to convey only the need for respecting "vested rights" and quiet possession: life, liberty, and the activities that were involved in the acquisition and possession of property were all of positive and dynamic character.

Often noted in commentary on the Constitution is the absence in the 1787 document of the reference, so prominent in Jefferson's language in the Declaration of Independence, to "pursuit of happiness." But it seems a fair reading of the Constitution's Preamble to say that "blessings of liberty" is a phrase that imported into the document the tone, at least some of the specific content, and certainly the general connotations of phrases in state constitutions and the Declaration pertaining to "happiness."[28] The degree to which liberty and its "blessings," the pursuit of happiness and the ideal of keeping the way open for the individualistic quest for acquisition of wealth (i.e., for maintaining a situation of open economic opportunity), are overlapping concepts is as much subject to reasonable disputation as, say, interpretation of "general welfare" or even "due process."[29] Jack Greene has explored the meaning of the notion of "happiness" in the Revolutionary and Founding era, for example, and contends very persuasively that this ideal transcended mere concern with security of private property. It had a meaning, Greene argues, which embodied dynamic economic liberty and also important public values:

> Peace and a situation in which citizens might become prosperous and achieve a state of what was referred to as "competency and independence" were said to be important components of happiness and legitimate goals of political society.[30]

Thus, in his *Rights of Man* (1792), Thomas Paine contended that "true happiness" had been discovered in America to be produced when every citizen had the right to "pursue his occupation, and enjoy the fruits of his labors, and the product of this property, in peace and safety, and with the least possible expense."[31]

That the notion of property itself—and its acquisition, and its relationship to the public happiness and blessing of liberty—was not confined, in the mind of republican theorists, to things material was evident also in a remarkable passage in one of James Madison's writings during the earliest years of the republic. Granting the Blackstone version of "property" as the bundle of rights that comprised one's private dominion over a tangible asset, Madison insisted that there was also a "larger and juster meaning," embracing things to which persons attached value and had rights but which (unlike dominion) did not require exclusion of others but rather "left to every one else the like advantage."[32] In this larger sense,

> a man has property in his opinions and the free communication of them. He has a property of peculiar value in his religious opinions, and in the profession and practice dictated by them. He has a property very dear to him in the safety and liberty of his person. He has an equal property in the free use of his faculties, and free choice of the objects on which to employ them. In a word, as a man is said to have a right to his property, he may be equally said to have a property in his rights.[33]

There was to be equality in this sort of "property in rights," then—and an equality in allowing citizens "free use of [their] faculties" was an expression that meant equality of opportunity—"the equal right of every citizen," as Greene says, "to pursue his happiness, to achieve the best life possible within the limits of his ability, means, and circumstances. . . ."[34]

The rhetoric of rights, equality, opportunity, happiness, and liberty is necessarily ambiguous; and so to draw inferences and connect ideas with great confidence is a misguided quest. Yet the direction of the Founding generation's thought on these matters—viewing property and rights in the terms Madison set out, embodying notions of economic liberty and opportunity; linking them with equality of rights; and setting forth the elements of fundamental liberties in terms that embraced not only property but its acquisition in the context of liberty, equality of opportunity, and rights—militates against an easy dismissal of "the blessings of liberty" phrase in the preamble as an open-ended generality. It was, it seems to me, a generality that resonated with ideals that embodied notions of both public good and privatistic interest, but above all notions of economic liberty.

The late nineteenth century and conservative constitutionalism

These ideas that we have just considered from the Founding generation, with respect to the rights of equal and open opportunity to acquire wealth and pursue happiness, were hardly strangers to the dialogue on American constitutional values after the Civil War. They reappeared in two distinct phases of the late nineteenth-century development of constitutional doctrine, being invoked, however, for very different purposes and with varying constitutional implications.

First, the ideals of equal opportunity were embodied in the movement for emancipation, finding expression at the very core of the "free labor" philosophy voiced in the abolitionist and Unionist movement in antebellum politics, then becoming central to the rationale for the Thirteenth and Fourteenth Amendments and for the programs of Reconstruction that included land, schools, and equal economic opportunity—all vital elements of economic liberty—for the freed blacks.[35] The interpenetration of equal rights with economic liberty in radical thought of the Civil War era was imprinted in no way more dramatically than in the postwar Civil Rights Act that complemented the Freedman's Bureau legislation with a general guarantee that "all citizens of the United States shall have the same right, in every State and Territory, as is enjoyed by white citizens thereof to inherit, purchase, sell, hold, and convey real and personal property," to make and enforce contracts, and to sue and give witness.[36] These rights of property and economic liberty for individuals in the marketplace were regarded as "fundamental rights which are the essence of civil freedom. . . ."[37] The purposes of the Civil Rights Act were severely confined and finally betrayed by a Supreme Court little concerned, after the passage of the years, with the rights of the black population. Nonetheless, the language—standing alongside the powerful phrases of the Fourteenth Amendment concerning "equal protection" and "due process" for all citizens—remained on the statute books in the same way as the language of the Declaration of Independence had endured in antebellum America throughout the period of slavery's perpetuation. Eventually these phrases and ideas proved "a tough nut to crack," as Lincoln had said of the 1776 Declaration, and the ideal of equality of all persons became a symbol of ideals not attained but not erased from the nation's conscience.[38]

A great irony inheres, of course, in the history of constitutional law during this era that spanned the end of Reconstruction to the early twentieth century: while the ideals of economic liberty failed to provide enduring guarantees to the freed blacks, they were mobilized in the rhetoric and doctrine of conservative jurists for purposes of sustaining a highly privatistic version of property rights and striking down important social and economic reform legislation. Importing the language of the Declaration of Independence into his reading of the Constitution's guarantees of due process and equal protection, for example, Justice Stephen Field as early as 1873 announced a doctrine of the "right to pursue a lawful calling." State legislatures, he insisted, were not free to establish in arbitrary ways barriers to entry into the common trades, violative of the "sacred right to labor."[39]

Justice Field may have been mobilizing evidence from history for his own polemical purposes, to be sure, but he was not altogether wrong on the facts: the Founding generation's concepts of "pursuit of happiness" and even of "property," as we have seen, did indeed leave room for the notion of freedom to pursue a calling and the rights of free persons to use their faculties for lawful purposes in fulfillment of their aspirations and potential. Indeed, as Professor Charles McCurdy has reminded us in his studies of Field's constitutional ideas, that conservative exemplar did not have to go back to the radical Thomas

Paine or even to Madison: the man in the White House who had appointed
him gave Field enough warrant for his view on economic liberty and individual rights to pursue a calling. Indeed the Union, McCurdy writes, had just
finished fighting a war which, in President Lincoln's words, had been a

> people's contest . . . for maintaining in the world that *form and substance*
> of government whose leading object is to elevate the condition of man; to
> lift artificial weights from all shoulders; to clear the paths of laudable
> pursuit for all; to afford all men an unfettered start and a fair chance in the
> race of life.[40]

The Supreme Court's conservative majority went farther, as it proved, than
the high priest Field was himself prepared to go in establishing barriers against
the police power as a source of infringement on private property rights. "Liberty of contract," full-blown in what is now commonly known as Lochner era
jurisprudence, established the Court as a censor of legislation in ways that did
violence to separation of powers and the heritage of respect for the legitimacy
of police regulation in both American and common law. Field's doctrinal formulations of property rights, expressed in the context of mythical individuals
standing sturdily alone and contracting with equals in the marketplace, are
what we remember. The manifest inaccuracy of the imagery in the new corporate America and the inadequacy of the legal constructs to deal with deeply-
rooted social tensions and often violent class strife discredited conservative
laissez-faire jurisprudence and eventually (in the New Deal era) brought
it down.[41]

Preferred freedoms, the lost ideal of economic liberty, and the "new property"
Doctrinaire arguments for economic liberty and protection of vested rights
came to a bad end in the New Deal era, when the dislocations, human
suffering, and widespread failure of business institutions during the Great Depression produced a crisis for the old constitutionalism. The extraordinary
range of policy innovations that produced the modern welfare and regulatory
state in the New Deal period was mirrored in a revolution in constitutional
law: the Commerce Clause fell as a barrier to national regulatory legislation,
federal administrative law recast the framework of labor relations and associated property rights, formerly unrestrained enterprises and industries came
under close regulation, agriculture was made a managed sector with basic deci-
sion-making taken out of the hands of individual owners as the trade-off for
income support, and a new program of unemployment, disability, and welfare
was set in place based on compulsory contributions where private contractual
arrangements and charity had previously been relied upon. Even while the old
conservative majority still controlled the Supreme Court, in 1934 Chief Justice

Charles Evans Hughes, no wild-eyed anti-capitalist radical, wrote the famous opinion that upheld a state-ordered mortgage-payment moratorium, casting into a new and hardly recognizable form the Contract Clause as John Marshall had interpreted it.[42] The Supreme Court, in another 1934 case, also laid to rest two staple doctrinal instruments that had long been wielded by the conservatives as protection for private property against regulation: the "economic due process" and "affectation with a public purpose" doctrines. "Neither property rights nor contract rights are absolute," the Court declared; "for government cannot exist if the citizen may at will use his property to the detriment of his fellows. . . ." To regulate property "in the common interest"—in this instance, to impose controls that effectively administered prices and allocated markets for fluid milk throughout the State of New York, a kind of intervention that went vastly beyond any legislative measures that came before antebellum courts for judgment on the limits of the police power—was not unwarranted interference with economic liberty of farmers, distributors, and retailers, nor did it violate constitutional protections for property.[43]

All this was enough, perhaps, to warrant Judge James Oakes' view that, in that era of expanding social and economic controls from Washington, "property rights were essentially confined to a legal dust bin"![44] But things went even more badly for property rights in their classic Lockean aspect as the Supreme Court moved toward regular application of the concept of "preferred freedoms." This formulation made its first formal appearance in the famed Carolene Products Case footnote of Chief Justice Stone. The burden of the concept was that any legislation which "restricts . . . political processes" such as censorship laws or acts controlling freedom of assembly, and any legislation affecting the fate of "discrete and insular minorities," would receive from the Court "more searching judicial inquiry" than other (less preferred) freedoms. In this latter category were, of course, private rights in property.[45] Thereafter the Court adhered steadily to a course by which it categorized property rights as different from personal rights; the classic Lockean view of "property [as] an attribute of a man's personality,"[46] gave way, and it was relegated to a lesser status in the system of constitutional priorities.

Contemplating the advent and career of this new constitutional double standard, the late Judge Learned Hand remarked: "Just why property itself was not a 'personal right,' no one took the trouble to explain."[47] Champions of the New Deal regulatory programs and related state-level interventionism, old-line Progressives who had long kept the property doctrines of the Stephen Field era under steady attack, the new Legal Realists who hammered skeptically at all the formalist constructs that had stood in the way of mobilizing law to deal with large-scale corporate firms and their role in twentieth-century American society—all accepted too quickly, perhaps, this conceptual separation of property rights from personal rights that Judge Hand so deplored.

Was the separation a piece of unfortunate judicial legerdemain, as Hand contended, which comported with neither accurate constitutional mandate nor social reality? Did making room in the scheme of constitutional values for the Depression-era and post-World War II period of vast technological change, population growth, and supercorporate economic power structure validate a move that let the legislative will trump not only the rights associated with laissez-faire orthodoxy and Franklin Roosevelt's intractable enemies, the "economic plutocrats," but also trump rights associated by Field, by Lincoln and the abolitionists before him, and by Madison, Paine, and Locke with the use of a man or woman's faculties, fulfillment of the whole person, open economic opportunity in the society at large as a communal dimension of "economic liberty" that still must have borne *some* relationship to protection of individual rights of ownership and use?

For a long time, these questions as a matter of liberty and *constitutional* warrant were set aside. Economic opportunity remained on the national agenda, perhaps more prominently than it had ever been, but as a matter of policy and not so much a matter of law. The policies were many; they were diverse; and they were debated and initiated at both levels of the federal system. If the Works Progress Administration, designed to provide opportunities for work to the unemployed in all manner of professions and skills, was emblematic of the Depression Era approach, then the flourishing of the state college and university movement (including the community colleges or "junior colleges") and the GI Bill of Rights and the student financial-aid programs since the 1960s are emblematic of later approaches. Insofar as economic liberty as a constitutionally grounded *right* came to the surface, it was in connection with legal actions to obtain for blacks (and, by extension, other minorities) equal access to institutions of higher education, application of the Fourteenth Amendment to invalidate restrictive racial covenants in real-estate transactions and title, and finally in the great public schools desegregation decisions of 1954 and after.

The issue of rights moved back into legislative halls in 1964, when Congress debated and finally passed over vehement opposition from segregationists and conservative constitutionalists the civil rights act that gave all persons access on an equal basis to places and facilities of public accommodation—a change whose opponents denounced not only in the harsh langugae of racism but also in the more genteel periods that set out the classical Lockean property-rights claims of the restaurant owners, hotel keepers, and others in service occupations who did not want to admit all customers on an equal basis.[48]

The identification (anew) of property rights as personal rights

The preferred freedoms doctrine had created what Justice Stewart later termed flatly a "false" asymmetry between constitutional guarantees and social realities: "Property does not have rights," Stewart countered,

> People have rights. . . . In fact, a fundamental interdependence exists be-
> tween the personal right to liberty and the personal right to property.
> Neither could have meaning without the other. [Hence] rights in property
> are basic civil rights. . . .[49]

This argument for restoring property rights to the main civil rights category—
this challenge to the long-prevailing "double standard" of the Court on judicial
scrutiny—forces a reconsideration of how property and its relationship to "economic liberty" fit into the scheme of fundamental values. It challenges, for
example, the approach embodied in Dworkin's famous essay "Taking Rights
Seriously," in which one of the leading modern legal philosophers raised all the
timeless problems of rights, consent, duties, and hierarchies of values without
once even mentioning the word "property," or scarcely adverting to "economic
liberty" or any variant thereof.[50]

The sit-ins of the 1960s in the South, and then the debate over the civil rights
act in 1963-1964, injected anew into the American political dialogue considerations of where one person's rights and liberties ended and another's began,
and how to reconcile conflicts in the face of the Fourteenth Amendment's then-
still-unredeemed promise. At just the same time, a revitalization of property
and liberty concerns came into the dialogue of legal scholarship and constitutional thought with the publication of Charles Reich's stunningly original articles on what he called "the new property."[51]

Reich's main target was paternalism—not far off the point which conservative apologists for economic individualism had been targeting for their fire
since Herbert Hoover set the theme in the 1932 election.[52] Whereas the Hoover-
style criticism had been premised on the desirability of restoring minimalist
government, Reich's premise was that the legal system ought to bestow entitle-
ments on a constitutionally guaranteed basis instead of bestowing largess at
the pleasure of society's elective rulers and administrators. He cited government contracts, Social Security benefits, occupational licenses, welfare and
other income programs, franchises, subsidies, access to the public domain and
other resources, and delivery of services as interdependent parts in an elaborate mechanism by which some were favored, others left outside the realm of
benefits and privileges, and still others held in thrall by procedural standards
difficult to meet or simply by governmental caprice.[53] The argument turned,
in the end, on a reconsideration of the then-established view (heir of the preferred freedoms' doctrine and New Deal jurisprudence) that property and liberty are separable, that property rights and personal rights are two different things. Reich offered a view of property that ran in the face of such separation, a view that carried overtones of Field, Lincoln, Madison, and Locke
on individualism:

> Property is a legal institution . . . [that] performs many different functions. One of these functions is to draw a boundary between public and private power. Property draws a circle around the activities of each private individual or organization. Within that circle, the owner has a greater degree of freedom than without. Outside, he must justify or explain his actions, and show his authority. Within, he is master, and the state must explain and justify any interference. . . .
>
> Thus, property performs the function of maintaining independence, dignity, and pluralism in society by creating zones within which the majority has to yield to the owner. Whim, caprice, irrationality, and "antisocial" activities are given the protection of law. . . . The Bill of Rights also serves this function, but while [it] comes into play only at extraordinary moments of conflict or crisis, property affords day-to-day protection in the ordinary affairs of life.[54]

Arguing that even the Bill of Rights would be of little use to a citizen without property—since it is property that gives the individual the will and power required for the independence that the Bill of Rights is intended to protect—Reich argued for a reformulation of the constitutional guarantees that are necessary to create true zones of privacy of individuals. The protection, he contended, lay partly in requiring procedural reform so that governmental largess could not be distributed with blatant unfairness or be withheld capriciously and arbitrarily. Beyond that, however, Reich contended that *entitlement* must become part of the new property; "to build an economic basis for liberty today," by buttressing the citizens' rights to the new property, would be the equivalent of the Homestead Act a century earlier, in its purposes.[55]

Reich's argument, paralleling the arguments of a decade earlier in Brown v. Board of Education on behalf of black students in segregated schools, stressed not only the material basis of "self-sufficiency of the individual," whether in a good education or in other respects, but also the larger matter of helping individuals achieve true autonomy and personal fulfillment. An example of the New Deal-style liberal position (or at least one variant of that position) which came under fire now from Reich and others on the left—as it had been under attack consistently since the 1930s from the right—was the argument by Professor Bernard Schwartz, in his mid-1960s treatise on the Constitution. Schwartz contended that

> [t]he typical man today finds his greatness [sic] not in himself and in what he does, but in the business or labor organization which he serves. It is his relationship to such organizations that gives rise to the most significant legal consequences that attach to his existence and activities. . . .
>
> In a very real sense, the true liberty of the individual may be promoted by restrictions that the society imposes upon him in his own interest.[56]

With the view put forward by Reich and others, constitutional discourse returned to the once-standard nexus of property, economic liberty and the pursuit of happiness, and the communal good—only this time addressed in terms that reflected a critique of the modern technological and corporate order, the bureaucratic state, and New Deal liberalism with its faith in the survival of individuality within the network of interventionist welfare and regulatory measures.[57]

To a remarkable degree, disputation touching on all the nuances and variants of "economic liberty," in constitutional law and philosophy of the last quarter century has proceeded on the agenda marked out by the Warren Court in Brown and by the new emphasis on personal "autonomy" introduced by Reich and other jurisprudential scholars in a complex fusion of political and psychological concepts of individuality, personal independence, and personhood.[58] It bespeaks the force and direction of these developments in law and constitutional discourse that the cluster of problems and of rights that have been variously associated with "economic liberty" since 1787 are now brought under the rubric, "Rights of Individual Autonomy," in the standard casebooks and texts in constitutional law classes. This does not mean that we have strayed, however, from the constitutional tradition: Madison's exposition on the concept of property in rights and rights in property could find a place very nicely, as inscription or text, in these newly recast chapters of our law books; so would Stephen Field's discourses on fulfillment of individualism and the right to pursue an occupation. Ironically, Franklin Roosevelt's arguments for WPA and Social Security would not be misplaced in one of these newly reorganized law books' chapters on autonomy, though the perilous balance of governmental paternalism and Madisonian (if not Lockean) individualism might be tilted a bit should FDR be represented in this way!

The pursuit of personal autonomy as a constitutional value intimately related to economic liberty, but derivative in formal constitutional terms from the Fourteenth Amendment's equal protection clause and the privileges and immunities doctrine, has been manifest in a series of important claims before the Supreme Court bench in the last two decades. The constitutional validity of residency requirements for eligibility to receive welfare assistance was at issue in Shapiro v. Thompson, a 1969 case in which the Supreme Court struck down this instrument for inhibiting interstate migration. In his opinion for the majority, Mr. Justice Brennan declared that the dictates of federalism and also "our constitutional concepts of personal liberty unite to require all citizens be free to travel throughout the length and breadth of our land." Although the case dealt with needy persons and their right to state assistance, Justice Brennan cast the decision in positive terms of economic liberty, portraying the process of an indigent's move from one state to another as the quest of a person seeking "to migrate, resettle, find a new job, and start a new life. . . ." The dream of economic opportunity, not the dole, was at the center of the portrait.[59] This focus was made even clearer by Justice Brennan in his opinion for the majority in a decision upholding the right of welfare clients to a hearing before termination of benefits. By meeting basic subsistence needs, he wrote in Goldberg v. Kelley (1970):

> welfare . . . can help bring within the reach of the poor the same opportunities that are available to others to participate meaningfully in the life of the community. . . . Public assistance, then, is not mere charity, but a means to 'promote the general Welfare, and secure the Blessings of Liberty to ourselves and our Posterity.'

Sharp disagreement appeared in the Court, however, when the Justices split in a Maryland welfare rights case the same year: in Dandridge v. Williams, the majority upheld the state's power to establish its standards of support and need, even though its rules might not be "wise" or as "just and humane a system" as might be desirable. In an impassioned dissent, Justice Marshall (joined by Brennan) deplored the majority's unwillingness to extend Fourteenth Amendment considerations when "the most basic economic needs of impoverished human beings" were at stake. A "subsistence existence" was surely the minimum that the Constitution required, they argued: they sought to bring "life" back into a relationship with "liberty" that stressed the importance of the basic minima for existence.[60]

Such arguments over the proper limits of protection for "personhood" and autonomy, reflecting the new concerns for economic liberty, were among the most divisive and bitterly argued on the Burger Court. The employment discrimination cases all bear directly on economic liberty considerations; the matter of whether a right to protection of one's personal reputation (with all its implications for the individual's ability to function in the marketplace, whether in the job market or in other capacities) extends to forbidding police from publishing unproven charges of shoplifting in an effective official "blacklist" publication; and, of course, the matter of education, on which the California state supreme court and the United States high court have handed down opposed rulings, California finding that school districts' financial resources must be roughly equal whereas the federal Supreme Court has found vast disparities acceptable, despite the impact on the education of the young and on their economic opportunities. In each of these instances, the property claims or "liberty" interests of some are put in the balance against new formulations of "economic liberty" for others.

The two landmark shifts in the basic law since the Founding—the Fourteenth Amendment's adoption and belated application, and the Hughes Court's "New Deal legacy" in constitutional doctrine—have not yet run their course, and there are vital issues of economic liberty still unresolved. Whether the right to subsistence and the right to gainful employment, for example, will in our day be regarded as constitutionally mandated is a question pressed by distinguished proponents yet far short of even a start toward resolution. A striking case in point was the report, in 1976, of the Academy of Political and Social Science committee on the bicentennial of independence, following a convocation on basic constitutional values of scholars, elective officials, and members of the public. The report unequivocally interpreted equality of opportunity, which was taken as basic to the Declaration of Independence's terms, as requiring

> certain minimal standards of decency for every person . . . [covering] housing, health education, and generally opportunities for human self-fulfillment. This may have been the single most important constitutional idea emerging from the three days of discussion. . . . Diversity would be permitted above the minimum, but the minimum would be provided for all.[61]

Professor Charles L. Black, Jr. reiterated this position in a paper last year. The elimination of poverty, he contended, is no more chimerical as a constitutional ideal than was incorporation of the First Amendment as a limitation upon the states some sixty years ago when the Supreme Court was still flatly denying its applicability. Congress should be seen as having an affirmative constitutional duty, he contends, "to move, by a general diffusion of welfare, to give life to a constitutional justice of livelihood, and so prepare the way for the 'Pursuit of Happiness'. . . ."[62]

Thus, concern for "autonomy" and liberty has been recast in modern liberal thought—at least by those who remain sympathetic with New Deal notions of public responsibilities and humane standards of minimum services and opportunities, but who have grown disillusioned with paternalism—so that many advocate a system of rights based on a reconstituted "new" property, linked to the Fourteenth Amendment's procedural requirements as well as its broader egalitarian mandate. Opposed to this new view of liberty and autonomy is the strong neo-conservative movement of our day, based on the classic Lockean view of autonomy; it has been championed by critics who see governmental intervention as almost unfailingly "inefficient" and (by that light) lacking in justification. The neo-conservatives interpret the constitutional mandates as to property protection in terms that would go back to Lochner and ignore altogether the social tensions and systematic failures of the laissez-faire economy that threw Lochner into disrepute; the most extreme neo-conservative elements even portray public taxation, eminent domain, and all police regulations as somehow equivalent (because they are "takings," it is claimed). This view, essentially ahistorical, resolutely ignores the distinctions that have been systematically made by American jurists since the early nineteenth century in regard to these three powers that impinge (in the name of public rights and welfare) on private property—distinctions which in fact are embedded in received civil and common-law doctrine no less than in historic American constitutional practice.[63]

A word must be said, in conclusion, about the more traditional rights in property—the owner's "absolute dominion," in the Blackstonian phrase, where neither the state nor other individual owners are permitted by the basic law to make intrusions or cause damage or loss. Neither in the field of eminent domain nor in that of the police power has there been any extensive reversal of the doctrines that gave legislative power and discretion wide play. Unlike welfare-state and modern regulatory-state issues, however, the classic police and eminent domain doctrines are rooted squarely in the practices and law of the early Republic, when "obligations" and not only "rights" of property were vigorously pursued and when "public rights" were asserted alongside Lockean precepts.[64] Scholars hostile to interventionism and wanting to leave market forces alone are championing a robust "indemnity theory" that would require compensation of private owners on a much broader basis—that is, championing a much more expansive doctrine of inverse condemnation—and thus temper the effects of state action on individuals harmed. The courts meanwhile struggle with the question—for example, in a land-use regulation case involving down-zoning of a valuable tract of land in Tiburon, California, on San Francisco Bay—of the extent to which the Fourteenth Amendment protects "expectations" as a key part of the bundle of rights in property.[65] Thus, the dilemma of drawing the line between police power action (with loss to individuals not compensable) and eminent domain or inverse condemnation (requiring compensation) persists in much the same conceptual framework as it did one hundred fifty years ago.[66]

Withal, balancing "economic liberty" values embodied in private ownership rights against the claims of the community and the Constitution's egalitarian warrant for "economic opportunity," and likewise balancing "rights of the public" against this entire congeries of private claims, remains at the heart of our constitutional dialogue today. Simplistic definitions of "vested rights" and "sacredness of property," no less than some of the shibboleths mobilized in defense of an unbridled governmental paternalism, can too easily do violence both to the historical heritage and to a fair reading of the cluster of values that are basic to the American constitutional order.

University of California, Berkeley

NOTES

1. I have reference to some recent studies—especially by Richard Epstein and by Bernard Siegan—that attempt to read into the original Constitution a concern for security of property rights that is exclusively for protection of vested claims; this neo-con-

servative scholarship, which puts aside too easily the other values inherent in the scheme of constitutional precepts, even seeks to revive as a valid reading of the Constitution and the Fourteeth Amendment the doctrines associated, at the high point of a conservative Supreme Court's hostility to social and economic regulation, with Lochner v. New York (1905). See discussion and critique of this new work, provided from the perspective of a scholar who contends for a neo-Lockean liberal alternative standard, in Rogers M. Smith, *Liberalism and American Constitutional Law* (Cambridge, Mass., 1985). I return to this scholarship *infra*, text at note 60.

Interestingly, the Roger Sherman draft (July 1789) that has been recently discovered in the Madison Papers did not include a due process provision bearing on takings or property rights. See full text in *The New York Times*, 29 July 1987, page 20.

2. See William M. Treanor, "The Origins and Original Significance of the Just Compensation Clause of the Fifth Amendment," *Yale Law Journal*, 94 (1985): 694-716. Also, Harry N. Scheiber, "Original Intent and the Fifth Amendment: The Takings Concept," a lecture presented at the Vanderbilt University School of Law, February 1987, to be published in 1988 in a Conference on Judicial Studies volume on the Bill of Rights Amendments, under title (tentatively) of *Original Intent and Constitutional Interpretation*.

3. See section that follows in text.

4. Edward S. Corwin, "The Basic Doctrine of American Constitutional Law," *Michigan Law Review*, 12 (1914): 247-276; cf. Stuart Bruchey, "The Impact of Concern for the Security of Property Rights on the Legal System of the Early American Republic," *1980 Wisconsin Law Review*, 1135-1158 (an extended essay focused on Corwin's contention that the quest for giving property rights security under the Constitution and the quest to firm up national power by the Founders and the Marshall court were "one and the same problem").

5. Bernard Schwartz, *A Commentary on the Constitution of the United States*, Part II: *The Rights of Property* (New York, 1965), 231. He goes on: "So far, in fact, did American law go in this respect that it was characterized as conferring virtually sovereign power in the property owner" (ibid).

6. John R. Commons, *Legal Foundations of Capitalism* (1924, reprinted Madison, Wisconsin, 1959), 328; see also, inter alia, my own study, "Public Rights and the Rule of Law in American Legal History," *California Law Review*, 72 (1984): 217-251.

7. Scheiber, "Law and the Imperatives of Progress: Private Rights and Public Values in American Legal History," *Nomos, XXIV: Ethics, Economics, and the Law*, ed. J. Roland Pennock and J. W. Chapman (New York, 1982), 303-320.

8. This is a main theme of much of the modern literature of constitutional and legal history. See, for example, the analyses of the tension between private vested rights and the pressures on law generated by rapid economic change, in Lawrence M. Friedman, *A History of American Law* (second edition, New York, 1986); Willard Hurst, *Law and the Conditions of Freedom in the Nineteenth Century United States* (Madison, Wisconsin, 1956); William E. Nelson, *Americanization of the Common Law: The Impact of Legal Change on Massachusetts Society, 1760-1830* (Cambridge, Mass., 1975); Morton Horwitz, *The Transformation of American Law, 1790-1860* (Cambridge, Mass., 1977);

Harry N. Scheiber, "The Road to *Munn*: Eminent Domain and Public Purpose in the State Courts," *Perspectives in American History*, 5 (1971): 327-402; Scheiber, "Public Rights and the Rule of Law," loc.cit.

9. 2 Dall. 304 (1795).

10. Stanley Katz has written of the Revolutionary generation that "the right to property was an unquestioned assumption. . . . To assert this is merely to assert that they were 18th-century men," but beyond that they regarded property ownership as "one of the bases of republican government." (Katz, "Thomas Jefferson and the Right to Property in Revolutionary America," *Journal of Law and Economics*, 19 [1976]: 469-470.)

11. 2 Dall. 304, 310 (1795). The courts generally interpreted eminent domain limitations in ways that favored the condemnor, (a) through a theory of offsets, which subtracted from the compensation all benefits to the other property of the person whose property was taken, and (b) through a fairly open-ended theory of "public use," which in many states made it coterminous with legislative discretion. (Scheiber, "Property Law, Expropriation, and Resource Allocation by Government, 1789-1910," *Journal of Economic History*, 33 [1973]: 232-251.)

12. See Leonard W. Levy, *The Law of the Commonwealth and Chief Justice Shaw* (Cambridge, Mass., 1954); Scheiber, "Public Rights and the Rule of Law." Cf. Smith, *Liberalism and American Constitutional Law*, 22-24 (on Lockean scheme of obligations and liabilities to regulation); also, Kent Newmyer's full biographical study, giving abundant attention to republicanism in relation to property rights, *Supreme Court Justice Joseph Story: Statesman of the Old Republic* (Chapel Hill, N.C., 1985).

For a fascinating analysis, recently published, of public rights, community welfare, and "publicness" in relation to property, historically and in contemporary law, see Carol M. Rose, "Comedy of the Commons," article in the *University of Chicago Law Review* 53, 1986: 711-781. Another valuable perspective on colonial and nineteenth-century concepts is provide in Kenneth J. Vandevelde, "The New Property of the Nineteenth Century: The Development of the Modern Concept of Property," *Buffalo Law Review*, 29 (1980): 325-366.

13. Scheiber, "Public Rights and the Rule of Law," passim.

14. Chancellor Kent's Opinion, in Hildreth, *The Boston Opposition to the New Law* (Boston, 1838), 242. On Kent's jurisprudence, see, inter alia, Newmyer, *Supreme Court Justice Joseph Story.*

15. Charles River Bridge Co. v. Warren Bridge Co., 36 U.S. 420 (1837). On this case, see Stanley I. Kutler, *Privilege and Creative Destruction: The Charles River Bridge Case* (Philadelphia, 1970).

16. Commonwealth v. Chapin, 5 Pick. 199, 203.

17. Chapman v. Kimball, 9 Conn. 38 (1831).

18. On great ponds and public rights, see the illuminating study of a great New Hampshire judge, by John Phillip Reid, *Chief Justice: The Judicial World of Charles Doe* (Cambridge, Mass., 1967), 356-364 et passim.

19. See, inter alia, J. R. T. Hughes, *The Governmental Habit*; Louis Hartz, *Economic Policy and Democratic Thought: Pennsylvania 1774-1860* (1948); Scheiber, "Public Ec-

onomic Policy and the American Legal System: Historical Perspectives," *1980 Wisconsin Law Review*, 1159-1189.

20. In this regard, too, that is, the legal system as a whole functioned in ways that "had less to do with protecting holdings than it had to do with protecting ventures." (Hurst, *Law and the Conditions of Freedom in the 19th Century U.S.*, 24.)

For a view of these processes that finds exploitation on a systematic basis, contrary to my own view of the record, which finds tensions and many conflicting patterns of winners and losers (Scheiber, "Public Rights and the Rule of Law"), see Horwitz, *Transformation*, passim; cf. McClain, "Legal Change and Class Interests: A Review Essay," *California Law Review*, 68 (1980): 382-397.

The evidence on constitutional debate, public rights, and developmental policy goals is considered for one important issue in pre-1860 politics in Scheiber, "The Transportation Revolution and American Law: Constitutionalism and Public Policy," *Transportation and the Early Nation* (Indiana Historical Society, 1982): 1-29.

21. As I have argued elsewhere, the "imperatives of progress" served as a validating canon when courts reviewed legislative measures in eminent domain and police power actions that were challenged by private property owners, both individual and corporate. It was a pragmatic standard that courts made over into a principled one—what Willard Hurst termed "instrumentalist" principles. (On the substantive issues and the historiography as well, see Scheiber, "Law and the Imperatives of Progress: Private Rights and Public Values in American Legal History," 303-320; and my overview, "The Public Purpose Doctrine," in Levy and Karst, *Encyclopedia of the Constitution* [1986] and, on Hurst's seminal contributions, Scheiber, "At the Borderlands of Law and Economic History," *American Historical Review*, 75 [1970]: 743-756.)

22. See, for example, the dissenting opinion in United States v. Butler, 297 U.S. 1 (1936).

23. Pennsylvania Declaration of Rights, 1776, in Bernard Schwartz, *The Roots of the Bill of Rights* (New York, 1971), 2: 264.

24. Ibid., 266, 274.

25. Ibid., 375.

26. Ibid., 284 (Maryland). North Carolina's 1776 Declaration of Rights had a more general provision against grants of special privilege, in Article II (ibid., 286).

27. Ibid., 237.

28. William B. Scott, *In Pursuit of Happiness: American Conceptions of Property from the Seventeenth to the Twentieth Century* (Bloomington and London, 1977), is a study of selected thinkers in American jurisprudence and politics on the concept of happiness in relation to property. Gordon Wood states, as to the Revolutionary period, that "[T]he important liberty in . . . [republican] ideology was public or political liberty. In 1776 the solution to the problems of American politics seemed to rest not so much in emphasizing the private rights of individuals against the general will as it did in stressing the public rights of the collected people against the supposed privileged interests of their rulers." (Wood, *The Creation of the American Republic, 1776-1787* [New York, 1969], 61.)

29. Admittedly, however, "due process" was a term of art in the law, in the same way as "high crimes and misdemeanors" and the First Admendment strictures regarding free speech and press. Hence analysis of these latter concepts tends to be pursued by quest for earlier common law and English constitutional meanings, as in the work of Leonard W. Levy on the First Amendment or of A. E. Dick Howard on concepts from Magna Carta. Our quest for meanings in the Preamble, as I argue in the text following, necessarily operates in much less certain rhetorical terrain, yet I think is a valid and important kind of inquiry.

30. Jack P. Greene, "Values and Society in Revolutionary America," *Annals of the American Academy of Political and Social Science*, No. 426 (July 1976): 62.

31. Quoted in ibid., 63.

32. "Property," *National Gazette*, March 1792, in *Mind of the Founder*, ed. Marvin Myers, 243.

33. Ibid. The construct has its parallels with Madison's earlier view of "interests," in *The Federalist*, No. 10. Since this study was written, an important work on Revolutionary era thought has appeared that treats exhaustively the issues of rights in property and property in rights: John Phillip Reid, *Constitutional History of the American Revolution* (Madison, Wisconsin, 1987).

34. Greene, "Values and Society," 64.

35. Eric Foner, *Free Soil, Free Labor, Free Men: The Ideology of the Republican Party before the Civil War* (New York, 1970), 11-39 et passim.

36. 1866 Civil Rights Act, codified in 42 U.S. C. sec. 1982.

37. Civil Rights Cases, 109 U.S. 3, 22 (1883).

38. The authors of the Declaration, Lincoln argued, "meant to set up a standard maxim for free society . . . constantly looked to, constantly labored for, and even though never perfectly attained, constantly approximated, and thereby constantly spreading and deepening its influence and augmenting the happiness and value of life to all people, of all colors, everywhere." (*The Lincoln-Douglas Debates of 1858*, ed. R. W. Johannsen [New York, 1965], 304). The various writings of Eric Foner, among other scholars, have explored this theme and its relationship to "free labor" and constitutionalism; see note 35 supra.

39. Slaughter House Cases, 16 Wall. 461 (U.S., 1873). In an opinion in 1884, also on the Louisiana slaughterhouse monopoly, Field contended that the privileges and immunities clause applied only to the individual's right to labor and not to protection of special privileges.

40. Lincoln, quoted in Charles McCurdy, "Justice Field and the Jurisprudence of Government-Business Relations: Some Parameters of Laissez Faire Constitutionalism, 1863-1897," in *American Law and the Constitutional Order*, ed. L. Friedman and H. Scheiber (Cambridge, Mass., 1978), 250.

41. McCurdy, "Justice Field," 265; see, inter alia, Earl Warren Legal Institute, *The New Deal Legacy and American Constitutional Law* (Boalt Hall School of Law Conference Proceedings, Berkeley, Calif., 1984).

42. The standard overviews are William Leuchtenburg, *Franklin D. Roosevelt and the*

New Deal, 1932-1940 (New York, 1963); and Paul Murphy, *The Constitution in Crisis Times, 1918-69* (New York, 1972). See also Scheiber, "American Federalism and the Diffusion of Power: Historical and Contemporary Perspectives," *University of Toledo Law Review*, 9 (1978): 619, 644-656. The mortgage suspension case mentioned is Home Building and Loan Association v. Blaisdell, 290 U.S. 398 (1934). Some commentators have heralded a revitalization of Contract Clause doctrine as the result of the decision in Allied Structural Steel Co. v. Spannaus, 438 U.S. 234 (1978); see Bernard Schwartz, "Old Wine in New Bottles? The Renaissance of the Contract Clause," 1979 *Supreme Court Review*, (1979) 95-121.

43. Nebbia v. New York, 291 U.S. 502 (1934). See Murphy, *Constitution in Crisis Times*, 113-114; and my essays on "Nebbia v. New York," on "Vested Rights," and on "Affected with a Public Interest," in *The Encyclopedia of the American Constitution.*

44. James L. Oakes, "'Property Rights' in Constitutional Analysis Today," *Washington Law Review*, 56 (1981): 608.

45. U.S. v. Carolene Products Co., 304 U.S. 144, 152-3 (1938). See Laurence H. Tribe, *American Constitutional Law* (Mineola, N.Y., 1978), 50-51 and chaps. 11-13, 15-16, passim.

46. Oakes, "'Property Rights,'" 585. See also Smith, *Liberalism and American Constitutional Law* (Cambridge, Mass., 1986); and essays by Malcolm Feeley, Lawrence M. Friedman, and myself, in Earl Warren Legal Institute, *The New Deal Legacy.*

47. Hand, "Chief Justice Stone's Conception of the Judicial Function," *Columbia Law Review*, 46 (1946): 698; see discussion in Oakes, "'Private Property,'" 585.

48. See Murphy, *Constitution in Crisis Times*, 363-364; Benjamin Muse, *Ten Years of Prelude* (New York, 1964). Also, on the Mexican American movement for civil rights in the Southwest, Ricardo Romo, "George I. Sanchez and the Civil Rights Movement, 1940-1960," *La Raza Law Journal*, 1 (1986): 342-362.

49. Lynch v. Household Finance Corp. 405 U.S. 538 (1972).

50. Dworkin, "Taking Rights Seriously," in *Is Law Dead?*, ed. Eugene V. Rostow (New York, 1971), 168-193. Dworkin did manage one reference, however, to having one's house burned as a problem of rights denied by the violent acts of others (ibid., 190).

51. Reich, "The New Property," *Yale Law Journal*, 73 (1964), reprinted in *American Law and the Constitutional Order*, ed. Friedman and Scheiber, 377-394. See also Arthur Selwyn Miller, *The Supreme Court and American Capitalism* (New York, 1968).

52. See Arthur M. Schlesinger, Jr., *The Age of Roosevelt: The Coming of the New Deal* (Boston, 1958).

53. Reich, "New Property," loc.cit., 337-384.

54. Ibid., 390.

55. Ibid., 394. Hope, myth, and reality in terms of how land policy, especially the Homestead Act, could and allegedly did (or did not) promote economic liberty through democratic landownership, is an interesting theme not pursued here. It is explored fruitfully, and with important bearing on the line of analysis I have tried to pursue, in Mary E. Young, "Congress Looks West: Liberal Ideology and Public Land Policy in the Nineteenth Century," *The Frontier in American Development: Essays in Honor of Paul Wal-*

lace Gates (Ithaca, New York, 1969), 74-112; Lawrence B. Lee, "The Homestead Act: Vision and Reality," *Utah Historical Quarterly*, 30 (1962); and Paul Wallace Gates, *History of Public Land Law Development* (Washington, 1968).

56. Schwartz, *A Commentary on the Constitution*, Part II, 205.

57. At about the same time, in the sixties, a strong challenge by economic historians of various viewpoints both to the established "liberal" view and the old-line "minimalist" views in their field of scholarship had some intriguing parallels to what was going on in legal scholarship in that era. Notably, Professor Hughes' book on government and the economy in American history and public law addressed the same issues as Reich did, from a posture largely critical of interventionism and modern giantism in government, yet a posture distinctly different from that of critics who advanced, wholesale, the orthodox arguments from the right against social intervention. This is another strand of modern intellectual history, and an interesting one, and I hope to pursue it on another occasion.

See Hughes, *Governmental Habit*; also, Hughes, "Transference and Development of Institution Constraints upon Economic Activity," *Research in Economic History*, ed. P. Uselding, 1 (1976). See also the insightful commentary by Willard Hurst, "Old and New Dimensions of Research in U.S. Legal History," *American Journal of Legal History*, 23 (1979): 1-20.

58. The "autonomy" theme has been accentuated, of course, and become the center of political firestorms as privacy and autonomy values were extended to embrace women's right to control the decision to carry a fetus or undertake abortion. For a narrower view, centering on a critique and extension of traditional property concepts, see Margaret Jane Radin, "Property and Personhood," *Stanford Law Review*, 34 (1982): 957-1016.

59. Shapiro v. Thompson, 394 U.S. 618 (1969).

60. Dandridge v. Williams, 397 U.S. 471 (1970).

61. *Annals*, No. 426, 73.

62. Black, "Further Reflections on the Constitutional Justice of Livelihood," *Columbia Law Review*, 86 (Oct. 1986): 1114. Professor Black's article appeared after the lecture on which this paper is based was given, in Spring 1986.

63. See notes 1, 66.

64. See text above at notes 12 to 21.

65. Agins v. Tiburon, 447 U.S. 245 (1980). See also Penn Central Transp. Co. v. City of New York, 438 U.S. 104 (1978); and San Diego Gas and Electric Co. v. San Diego, 450 U.S. 621 (1981). In June 1987 the Court established a new doctrinal basis for judicial review of the inverse condemnation issue, requiring compensation if state-imposed delays imposed unreasonable costs. First English Evangelical Church v. Los Angeles, 107 Sup. Ct. 2378 (1987).

66. See Joseph L. Sax, "Some Thoughts on the Decline of Private Property," *Washington Law Review*, 58 (1983): 481-496; William B. Stoebuck, "A General Theory of Eminent Domain," *Washington Law Review*, 47 (1972): 553-608; and, for a singularly ahistorical critique of takings law based on a doctrinaire, negative view of the legiti-

macy of redistribution of wealth by government, Richard Epstein, *Takings: Private Property and the Power of Eminent Domain* (Cambridge, Mass., 1985). See also the full critical discussion of the related public trust concept, in Richard J. Lazarus, "Changing Conceptions of Property and Sovereignty in Natural Resources," *Iowa Law Review*, 71 (1986): 631-716; the seminal statement of the position Lazarus criticizes, in Joseph L. Sax, "The Public Trust Doctrine in Natural Resource Law: Effective Judicial Intervention," *Michigan Law Review*, 68 (1970): 471-491; and also the historical survey and analysis by Molly Selvin, "The Public Trust Doctrine in American Law and Public Policy, 1789-1920," *1980 Wisconsin Law Review*, 1403-1442.

The School Prayer Controversy in America: Constitutionalism, Symbolism, and Pluralism

by Stanley I. Kutler

"[I]f My people who are called by My name humble themselves and pray and seek My face, and turn from their wicked ways, then will I hear from heaven, and forgive their sin and heal their land."

2 Chronicles 7:14

"And when you lift up your hands, I will turn My eyes away from you; though you pray at length, I will not listen. Your hands are stained with crime—Wash yourselves clean; Cease to do evil; learn to do good. Devote yourselves to justice; and the wronged. Uphold the rights of the orphan; Defend the cause of the widow."

Isaiah 1:15-17

"You go to your church, and I'll go to mine."

American aphorism

Shall we sing the Lord's song in the public schools? As spring approached in 1984, that question briefly monopolized political discourse in the United States. The massive effort for a constitutional amendment to permit organized, vocal prayers in the schools marked another in a long series of attempts to reverse the Supreme Court's 1962 ruling in Engel v. Vitale that prohibited schoolroom prayers prescribed and written by the New York Board of Regents.[1]

Ronald Reagan's "social agenda" in the 1980 presidential campaign included restoring public school prayers as well as halting abortions and racially-mandated school busing. On the prayer issue, fundamentalist and evangelical groups generated formidable enthusiasm, supported by public opinion polls demonstrating that more than eighty percent of the American people favored prayer in the public schools. Candidate Reagan, of course, became President Reagan, and early in 1984, he sought to redeem his campaign promises (and prepare for the next one) as he vigorously lobbied for a constitutional amendment.

The public debate of 1984 was like the sight of a shooting star: intense, stunning, and yet ephemeral. Political observers had to wonder at the allocation of political energies devoted to the prayer issue, while at the same time, public interest was languid at best regarding the American involvement in Lebanon and Central America, the escalating budget deficit, the lack of progress towards arms controls, and the ethical behavior of public officials. And on further reflection, one also had to wonder whether the dramatic clash over the proposed amendment represented genuine constitutional concerns or merely a stylized routine to provide an overture for America's quadrennial ritual of presidential elections.

President Reagan's public statements in behalf of the prayer amendment illustrate the art and practice of symbolic politics; nevertheless, the pro-prayer movement should not be dismissed lightly. The recent turmoil, as well as the preceding two decades of agitation, reflects significant constitutional questions, questions that go to the very heart of American traditions of religious liberty; questions that compass the very nature of contemporary American pluralism; questions that reveal dangerous, maybe even irreconcilable tensions in the American social fabric. The prayer issue mirrors conflicts and values deeply ingrained in American history. In turn, the controversy has resurrected old issues—issues of separation of church and state, conflicts between competing strains of faith and secularism, and clashes between traditionalism and modernism, and with all the attendant ingredients of alienation and disaffection.

The prayer controversy is richly laced with history, much of it, however, distorted or forgotten by partisans on both sides. Schoolchildren learn that American history began partly as a search for religious freedom, most notably with the Puritan experience in Massachusetts. But they also usually (or should) learn that the Puritans themselves became oppressors and demanded rigid conformity much as they had resisted in England. In short, the struggle for social peace in the midst of a pluralistic society lies rooted in early American history.

As colonies became a diverse nation, the pluralist dilemma led to a pluralist solution. In 1791, James Madison, fresh from his conflicts with established religion in Virginia, and deeply troubled by the prospects of state-supported religious activities, incorporated a provision on church-state separation into the First Amendment: "Congress shall make no law respecting an establishment of religion, or prohibiting the free exercise thereof. . . ." The fact that the phrases on religion precede similar proscriptions against congressional interference with speech, the press, assembly, and petition may well indicate the importance of the matter to Madison and others.[2]

Thomas Jefferson's oft-quoted metaphor on separation has dominated the constitutional and historical understanding of the First Amendment guarantee. "I contemplate with sovereign reverence," he wrote to a group of Connecticut Baptists in 1802, "that act of the whole American people which declared that their legislature should 'make no law respecting an establishment of religion or prohibiting the free exercise thereof,' thus building a wall of separation between church and state."[3]

Jefferson's judgment, a reflection of contemporary enlightened rationalism, was largely political. But we often overlook the religious, particularly evangelical, impetus for separation. Here the roots again extend back to Puritan Massachusetts and Roger Williams' challenge to orthodoxy and establishment. Williams spoke of the need to maintain "a wall of separation between the garden of the church and the wilderness of the world." Unlike Jefferson, the Reverend Mr. Williams feared the corrupting influence of the state upon religion, an essentially theological judgment. The same fears animated the Great Awakening.[4] And, as we shall see, some influential religious leaders and institutions continue to base their First Amendment commitment on Williams' theological, rather than Jefferson's political concerns.

During his American travels in the 1830s, Alexis de Tocqueville was deeply impressed with what he called the "religious aspect" of the country. The Catholic Frenchman, of course, was bewildered by the multiplicity of sects, but even more by the relatively peaceful relations among differing American religious groups. Catholic priests repeatedly told him that the separation of church and state was the key. "In America religion is a distinct sphere," Tocqueville wrote, "in which the priest is sovereign, but out of which he takes care never to go."[5]

Tocqueville's usual perceptiveness was a bit shortsighted. While church-state separation was a reality on the national level—despite Congress's (over Madison's objections) authorization of chaplains for itself and the military, and for allowing census takers to note the number of ministers in the nation— the First Amendment offered no barrier against state governmental intrusions in the religious sphere. South Carolina's constitution of 1778 made "the Christian Protestant religion" the "established religion," and guaranteed equal religious and civil privileges to Christian Protestants—and apparently only to Christian Protestants. The Boston public schools required schoolchildren to recite the Ten Commandments and the Lord's Prayer. Catholic immigrant children, under orders from their priests, refused and were disciplined with the rod. State courts upheld the practice on the grounds that the Bible usefully inculcated the young with "principles of piety, justice, and a sacred regard to truth, love of their country, humanity, and a universal benevolence, sobriety, moderation and temperance, and those other virtues which are the ornaments of human society, and the basis upon which a republican constitution is founded."[6]

The nineteenth-century experience was harshest for Tocqueville's Catholic co-religionists. "Moral education" long had been a fixture in the common schools. Horace Mann believed that if public schools were to attract all children they had to provide a common core of religious belief. "Moral education," he said, "is a primal necessity." The core belief was simple: there is but one God, we are dependent upon Him, and we are sinners, but God in his mercy had provided a savior in Jesus Christ. But this really meant a kind of pan-Protestantism for the classroom as the so-called "universal Christian truths" usually reflected particular Protestant liturgies.[7]

Nationalism, as well as religious truth, was at stake for the Protestant majority. As Catholic immigrants flooded the Northeast in the mid-nineteenth century, nativists eagerly used the common schools as a forum to "Americanize" immigrant children and to subject them to the dominant religious and social values. Catholic priests realized that the First Amendment had no self-enforcing injunctions; accordingly, they mobilized their parishioners to resist Protestant domination. Sometimes, Catholics overthrew the sectarian impositions through political force, as in New York; in Wisconsin, Catholics persuaded the state court to strike down required Bible-reading in the schools as a violation of state constitutional requirements of separation.[8]

Most states constitutionally required separation, but seemingly without contradiction most also required their schools to promote religious and moral values. The Kansas Supreme Court encountered that conflict in the early twentieth century, and its resolution offers some insights into the dilemma.

The Quincy school in Topeka, Kansas regularly began the school day with students reciting the Lord's Prayer and the 23rd Psalm. Philip Billard's father objected, claiming that he "conscientiously opposed" the practice because it constituted a form of religious worship. Accordingly, the school board excused young Philip from participating and authorized him to enter the classroom following the ritual. Billard *fils* must have been a budding young scholar for he (or his father) insisted on his right to be at his desk during this period, and to study while the others participated in the prayer readings. The authorities expelled Philip after repeated admonitions and confrontations.

Billard *père* filed suit, contending that the readings represented unconstitutional religious exercises. He cited the state bill of rights which provided that no person could be compelled to attend or support any form of worship, a state constitutional provision prohibiting religious sects from controlling any public school funds, and finally, a 1901 statute stipulating that "no sectarian or

religious doctrine shall be taught or inculcated in any of the public schools."
Unfortunately, Billard's lawyer covered only half of the statute, for the 1901
law also provided that "nothing in this section shall be construed to prohibit
the reading of the Holy Scriptures."

The Topeka case was 1904, not 1984; the setting was the Kansas Supreme
Court and the First Amendment of the United States Constitution was not at
issue. The Kansas court conceded that the state could not promote sectarian or
religious doctrines. But in that age the court had no difficulty in finding significant secular qualities in the Bible. State constitutional doctrine required
schools to "encourage the promotion of intellectual, moral, scientific, and agri-
cultural improvement." Students were expected to learn right from wrong, as
well as the higher ideals of life. And how could this be done? "The noblest
ideals of moral character are found in the Bible," the court declared. "To emu-
late these is the supreme conception of citizenship." The Billards clearly
learned a lesson in majoritarianism. Whatever legal and constitutional arguments they could raise in behalf of their position, they had to confront a court
that believed that Bible-reading promoted more than just religion.

The Kansas case provided a useful precedent for latter-day advocates of
prayer, Bible-reading, and moments of silence who contend that such exercises
have non-sectarian purposes. The lower court trial record persuaded the apel-
late judges that the prayer exercise was designed "to prepare the children for
their work, to quiet them from the outside." The court further found that the
teacher betrayed no effort to inculcate religious dogma. She merely sought to
"quiet" the children; she made no responses, comments, or remarks about the
religious passages. Pupils were free to let their minds wander. The only demand of the civil authority was that all students behave themselves. Young
Philip's attempts to study during prayer recitation apparently was disorderly.
In short, it was a breach of discipline case; in that more authoritarian, less
litigious, age, one in which the understanding of federalism precluded federal
courts from applying the First Amendment against state action, the Billards'
cause was hopeless.[9]

The Kansas decision naturally reinforced those who desired a religious component to moral education. But by the early twentieth century, many educa-
tors realized that it was "impossible to make a generalization of Christianity";
furthermore, many understood that some religious activities violated constitutional requirements of separation and trivialized religion. Meanwhile, the ac-
celerating diversity of Americans hastened the professionals' revolt against
religiously-oriented moral education and toward a concept of religious neutrality. In time, "moral education" developed into new lessons regarding racial,
sexual, and cultural equality, and the potential for humans—in short, what
one historian of education has called "cosmopolitan solutions" for a pluralistic
system.[10]

"Scarcely any question arises in the United States that is not resolved, sooner or later, into a judicial question." Tocqueville's familiar maxim has been particularly true for civil rights and civil liberties conflicts. In the last half century, the United States Supreme Court has confronted a wide range of such questions, and with varying results. But the most significant outcome has been the nationalization of the Bill of Rights, as the Court has applied the Fourteenth Amendment to protect individuals against state infringement of those freedoms guaranteed in the federal constitution. In Cantwell v. Connecticut (1940) the Court held the religion clause of the First Amendment to be within the purview of the Fourteenth.[11]

A more decisive ruling came in the Everson case in 1947. Curiously, a majority of the justices sustained the constitutionality of state-provided transportation to parochial school children while vigorously advancing Jefferson's "wall of separation" metaphor. Although some justices believed that busing breached the wall, all generally agreed with Justice Hugo Black's majority statement on the meaning of the First Amendment:

> The "establishment of religion" clause of the First Amendment means at least this: Neither a state nor the Federal government can set up a church. Neither can pass laws which aid one religion, aid all religions, or prefer one religion over another. Neither can force nor influence a person to go to or to remain away from church against his will or force him to profess a belief or disbelief in any religion. No person can be punished for entertaining or professing religious beliefs or disbeliefs, for church attendance or non-attendance. No tax in any amount, large or small, can be levied to support any religious activities or institutions, whatever they may be called, or whatever form they may adopt to teach or practice religion. Neither a state nor the Federal government can, openly or secretly, participate in the affairs of any religious organizations or groups and vice versa. In the words of Jefferson, the clause against establishment of religion by law was intended to erect "a wall of separation between Church and State."[12]

Following Everson the Court vacillated in its commitment to an absolute wall of separation. It struck down released-time programs for religious instruction on school property, approved a similar one off school grounds, upheld Sunday closing laws, and struck down a state ruling denying unemployment compensation to someone who refused to work on her Sabbath. Little wonder, then, that when the Court announced its 1962 ruling striking down state-sponsored school prayers in New York, its inconsistency "reaped the scorn of a confused and aroused public."[13] But the Court's decision in Engel v. Vitale, supported by six of the seven sitting justices, invoked principled constitutional arguments; given the facts, the issue of church-state separation could not have been more clearly joined.

The New York Board of Regents is a government agency with broad executive and legislative powers over the state's educational system. As part of its "Statement on Moral and Spiritual Training in the Schools"—a recognition of its responsibilities to offer such a program—the Regents included a prayer for daily classroom use:

> Almighty God, we acknowledge our dependence upon Thee, and we beg Thy blessings upon us, our parents, our teachers, and our Country.

The Regents conceded that the prayer was religious, but also argued that the nation's spiritual heritage justified its use.

Justice Black, again speaking for the Court, relied heavily on the Jeffersonian-Madisonian political solution to build his case for separation, as he had in Everson. Black's view of American colonial history and the background to the First Amendment convinced him that the New York Regents' prayer violated the Establishment Clause of the First Amendment. The Justice found the prayer to be nothing less than a "religious activity." As such, it was forbidden by the Establishment Clause which at a minimum meant for Black that "in this country it is not part of the business of government to compose official prayers for any group of the American people to recite as part of a religious program carried on by government." The non-compulsory stipulation did not, Black argued, alter the unconstitutionality of the Regents' action.[14]

Black saw constitutional arrangements as supportive, not destructive, of religion and religious liberty. The Puritan repression and unhappy colonial experiences with establishment, he believed, had sensitized Americans to the dangers of church-state union. With the revolution and independence, Americans deliberately removed numerous vestiges of state-established religious institutions and functions. The Establishment Clause of the First Amendment formalized the process; its purpose, as Black succinctly noted, "rested on the belief that a union of government and religion tended to destroy government and to degrade religion."[15] Finally, Black cemented Thomas Jefferson's "wall of separation" to better protect Roger Williams' "garden" against the encroachment of the "wilderness": "It is neither sacrilegious nor anti-religious to say that each separate government in this country should stay out of the business of writing or sanctioning official prayers and leave that purely religious function to the people themselves and to those the people choose to look to for religious guidance."[16]

A year later, in Abington Township v. Schempp, the Court struck down a Pennsylvnia statute directing that "at least ten verses from the Holy Bible" be read daily in the schools. The Court, particularly through Justice Brennan's lengthy concurring opinion, spoke more elaborately on the issue of religion in the public schools, but the doctrinal thrust remained essentially the same as in Engel.[17]

Two days after the Engel ruling, President John F. Kennedy deftly defended the decision in his nationally-televised press conference. "We have in this case a very easy remedy," the president said, "and that is to pray ourselves. We can pray a great deal more at home, we can attend our churches with a good deal more fidelity, and we can make the true meaning of prayer much more important in the lives of our children. I would hope that as a result of this decision, all American parents will intensify their efforts at home, and the rest of us," he concluded, "will support the constitution and the responsibility of the Supreme Court in interpreting it."[18]

The senior American Catholic prelate, however, sharply disagreed. For Cardinal Francis Spellman, the decision struck "at the very heart of the Godly tradition in which America's children" had been raised. Protestant evangelical Billy Graham protested that the decision constituted "another step toward the secularization of the United States." Even traditionally liberal Protestant leaders such as Reinhold Niebuhr and Bishop James A. Pike attacked the decision. Liberal Senator Eugene McCarthy, a Catholic, concurred with Graham, saying that the decision promoted "a secularized society." Other congressional responses were blunter. A southern congressman complained that the Supreme Court had "put the Negroes in the schools and now they've driven God out." Another complained that the decision followed communist lines.[19]

The prominent journals of opinion reacted predictably. The *Christian Century*, a liberal Protestant periodical, quickly distanced itself from fundamentalist Protestants. The organ pointed out that personal, private prayer—"the kind of prayer honored in Scripture and most often practiced"—was untouched by the Court's ruling. Seeing the separation principle as benefiting organized religions, the journal praised the decision for thwarting those who sought to use official power "to enforce conformity to religious or political ideas." Finally, the *Christian Century* sharply criticized Billy Graham when it asked: "Since when do Christians run to the government to save God?" The New York Regents, not the Court, it argued, had secularized the nation by writing a meaningless, trivialized prayer.[20]

The liberal Catholic publication, *Commonweal*, reacted with confusion and ambivalence. Acknowledging that "Engel v. Vitale was neither radical nor strained," the journal nonetheless criticized the Court for ignoring the majority's traditions and customs. Religion undeniably had a place in American life, *Commonweal* said, and "a genuine pluralism must, however, recognize the importance of the majority too." Significantly, the journal acknowledged that the Court and the American people did not know how to reconcile majority and minority rights.[21] And nowhere did *Commonweal* offer any insight into what constituted the "majority" and the "minority" in American life.

Other Catholic publications offered more scathing criticism. The *Catholic World*, a Paulist publication, complained that the Court had employed "absolute legal theory" to subvert "a cherished and highly serviceable system of

Church-State co-operation." The Jesuits' *America* bluntly called the decision "asinine," "stupid," "doctrinaire," "unrealistic," and one that "spits in the face of our history, our traditions, and our heritage as a religious people."[22]

The Jesuits obliquely complained about "the clamorous and constant protestations of a well-organized and litigious minority." They made the message more direct two months later. An editorial, entitled "To Our Jewish Friends," criticized Jewish "militants" and warned that Jews might suffer great losses leading to "social and cultural alienation" if they won all the "legal immunities" they sought. Jews had to decide what "bargain" they could strike as a minority in a pluralistic society.[23] Strangely, the Catholic commentary made no reference to the discrimination Catholics had suffered in the public schools.

Leonard W. Levy defended the Court's historical understanding, although he criticized its earlier decisions on religion as erratic and temporizing. The prayer decision, Levy argued, was historically and constitutionally sound, and he demonstrated how it reinforced the intentions of the First Amendment.[24] Levy's article appeared in *Commentary*, published by the American Jewish Committee, and partly answered the Jesuit attack on the decision. The AJC later responded directly to the Jesuits' "advice" to their "Jewish friends," defending what it considered to be a "Jewish position" on the matter of schoolroom prayers. Meanwhile, the arch-conservative *National Review* extended the Catholic-Jewish split, with Catholic editor William Buckley warning that anti-Semitism would increase if Jews weren't "careful."[25]

The prayer decision unleashed powerful attacks on the Supreme Court; more important, it provided an outlet for channeling deeply-felt religious sentiments in the nation. For the next two decades, an ostensible decline in religious faith and practice offered a convenient explanation for America's social ills. Well-organized, well-financed religious groups exploited the controversy to augment their numbers and to vent their moral concerns. Yet the response seemed exaggerated. Anthony Lewis, the *New York Times'* legal correspondent, shrewdly observed that the revolutionary reapportionment case, Baker v. Carr, decided only a few weeks before Engel, provoked relatively far less protest and outrage, save by long-established vested interests truly endangered by the decision. "It is ironic," Lewis wrote, "that a case with so much less potential for real change in our country's political and social structure—the Prayer case—has provoked so much greater outcry."[26]

Following the Engel decision, the Gallup Poll reported that 80% of its respondents approved religious observances in the public school while 14% disapproved. But the question was vague, as it merely inquired about "religious observances," and not about prayer or about any prayer in particular. A year later the public disapproved the Schempp decision by a 70-24 margin. The sample responses were predictable. Those who disagreed with the decision asked: "What's wrong with reading a prayer in school?"; "Prayer never hurt anybody"; "Children need religion at school because they don't get it at home"; "It's another step toward putting God out of everyday life." For others, however, "Religion should not be forced on people of different faiths"; "The place for religion is in the church and home, not in the schools"; "Church and State should be separated."

When the prayer issue was raised in the 1980 election, 76% of those responding favored a constitutional amendment permitting school prayer. Two years later, after significant presidential support of the idea, and with the heavily publicized activities of religiously-oriented pressure groups such as the "Moral Majority," the figure had risen another three points. Eighty per cent of those queried were aware of the proposed amendment. Despite the high percentages in favor of an amendment, a 1979 survey significantly revealed that 75% named the home, 16% the church, and only 3% the schools as most crucial to a child's religious and spiritual development.

Public opinion polls consistently demonstrate that approximately 95% of the American people "believe in God." (Similar polls in Italy, the Benelux countries, and Japan showed adherence scores of 88%, 78%, and 38%, respectively.) Only slightly more than half of the Americans polled, however, acknowledged that their religious beliefs were "very important" to them. Further probing reveals some interesting commitment to church-state separation. In the 1980 election, Cardinal Humberto Medeiros of Boston circulated a letter declaring it sinful to vote for pro-abortion candidates. By a 2-1 margin, one poll's respondents registered their disapproval of the Church's interference. (The result was similar for a general question regarding the organized efforts of religious groups to defeat particular candidates.) Reagan supporters disapproved of the Medeiros letter, 59-30%, and Carter's followers opposed it, 62-26%. But a month later, a Gallup Poll commissioned by *Christianity Today* found that nearly half of the respondents believed it either "very" or "fairly" important for religious organizations to speak out on political and economic matters as they see those issues consistent with the will of God. The general question fared much differently from the focused one.

The framing of a question can shape the results. Consider the abortion controversy, another issue raised and agitated largely by religious groups. Shortly after the Supreme Court approved limited abortions in 1974, public opinion supported the ruling by a narrow 47-44% margin. Seven years later, the figures were slightly reversed, standing at 45-46%. Clearly, opinion remained almost evenly divided. But re-wording the question resulted in dramatic changes. A 1981 ABC/*Washington Post* survey asked: "Should a woman be able to get an abortion if she decides that she wants one no matter what the reason?" A decisive 59% of the respondents disagreed. Shortly afterward, a CBS/*New York Times* poll asked: "Do you approve of an abortion if the woman wants to have it and the doctor agrees?" In this case, 63% replied affirmatively.

Unfortunately, we do not have any similar in-depth polling on the prayer issue. No questions on prayer have been shaped in the context of either a sophisticated or a vague understanding of the traditions of church-state separation. No Gallup poll posed the precise questions of Engel v. Vitale, which, after all, go to the heart of the issue. The issue is not a child's right to pray if he or she desires—indeed, as long as there are history exams, students probably will pray. Quite simply, people have not been asked whether they want a teacher to direct the reading of a government-written prayer. Perhaps a majority might respond affirmatively; but given the ambivalence of Americans toward the role of organized religion and its proselytizing effects, the response probably would not be anywhere near the 80% affirmative range evoked by the simple question of whether one favors prayer in the public schools.[27]

Notwithstanding the public outcry and inevitable *argumenta ad horrendum*, the Court's rulings did not strike down patriotic exercises that referred to God or acknowledged a dependence upon a Supreme Being. The decisions did not affect the singing of the fourth stanza of the Star-Spangled Banner, the reading of the Declaration of Independence, or the slogan "In God We Trust" which is engraved on coins. The Bible still could be read in schools for its literary and historical qualities, and religion still could be studied in its comparative aspects and as a historical phenomenon.[28] The Supreme Court had killed neither religion nor God. Congress, however, hedged its bets as the House of Representatives installed a plaque, incribed with "In God We Trust," over the Speaker's Chair. A later attempt to do the same for the Supreme Court's chamber, however, was quietly quashed.[29]

Yet political realities dwarfed the legal and textual precision that could be drawn out of the Engel and Schempp cases. The immediate congressional criticism was predictable; but the issue persisted and Senator Barry Goldwater raised it during the 1964 presidential election. Moral decay had accelerated as moral values had declined, crime and juvenile delinquency had increased, while anarchy and rebelliousness pervaded the society, the Senator exclaimed; "is this the time," he asked rhetorically, "for our Federal Government to ban Almighty God from our school rooms?"[30] Over time, Goldwater's 1964 statement proved to be the clarion call for the mobilization of pro-prayer forces. Yet in 1984, free from his constituency and consistent with his conservative faith, Senator Goldwater voted against a proposed constitutional amendment to allow prayer in the public schools.

The political assaults against the Court were fairly predictable, but the hostility could be traced partly to the Court's own inconsistency. After Engel, the judiciary "reaped the scorn of a confused and aroused public because it [had] been inconsistent," as Leonard Levy has argued. The compromised results of decisions such as the New York released-time case, the New Jersey busing decision, and the upholding of the Massachusetts blue laws differed from the principled ruling of Engel.[31]

For two decades following the prayer and Bible-reading decisions, the Court consistently adhered to the principles established in those cases. Most notably, in Lemon v. Kurtzman (1971), the Supreme Court devised a three-pronged test for measuring statutes and administrative actions against the dictates of the establishment clause. The act in question, the Court said, must have a clearly secular legislative purpose, its primary effect must neither advance nor inhibit religion, and it must avoid excessive governmental entanglement with religion.[32]

The post-Engel rulings have involved a variety of questions relating to religious matters and the public schools. For example, it is unconstitutional to require posting of the Ten Commandments in classrooms, whether or not there is official funding;[33] state salary supplements for parochial school teachers have been rejected;[34] state maintenance and repair aid to parochial elementary and secondary schools have been forbidden, but the use of state bonds to finance construction of a Baptist college was held to have a secular purpose;[35] teachers or professors who insist on leading prayers or Bible-reading may be dismissed since their actions violate the establishment clause;[36] schools may not use a prayer as its "pep song" and put it on walls or sing it at athletic contests;[37] a variety of rulings have struck down various attempts to establish "voluntary" prayer and Bible-reading sessions, in all of which the courts have held voluntariness irrelevant to the constitutional issue;[38] and required moments of silence generally have been struck down, particularly when the legislative history demonstrates that the statute's primary purpose involved the promotion of religious exercises.[39]

Such judicial rulings sometimes have produced disdainful reactions. The prohibition against the posting of the Ten Commandments even provoked bitter recriminations among the judges themselves.[40] When a court struck down a teacher-led recitation of the familiar refrain, "We thank you for the flowers so sweet, we thank you for the food we eat, we thank you for the birds that sing, we thank you for everything," there was not only division, but public and political scorn.[41] Actually, the courts have resisted a good deal of extremism. For example, they have upheld invocations and benedictions at high school graduation ceremonies;[42] the clause "under God" in the Pledge of Allegiance;[43] the carrying of religious items in space capsules;[44] that the phrase "so help me God" does not exclude atheists and agnostics from juries;[45] and that the use of phrases such as "In God We Trust" involves a patriotic and ceremonial exception that does not violate the establishment clause.[46]

But was the principled stand in Engel and its progeny too late? Were religious norms and forms, however diluted (or trivialized) firmly enshrined as part of the American pluralistic consensus? "We are a religious people whose institutions presuppose a Supreme Being," Justice Douglas wrote in the New York released-time case.[47] Douglas may have regretted that statement in later years; but that does not detract from its validity in 1952—or thirty-five years later. Such belief, however shadowy or imprecise personal commitments might be, is readily apparent. Understandably, then, given the constant tensions of a world on the brink of holocaust, was it not a patriotic duty that we—including our school children—acknowledge our faith and dependence on Almighty God? For a society subject to dramatic social strains and cultural shifts, for many it was imperative to maintain a familiar anchor. If so, the first order of business was a reversal of the Supreme Court's prayer decisions.

Proponents of school prayers have concentrated their efforts on a constitutional amendment to reverse the Engel and Schempp rulings. More than fifty amendments were proposed in Congress within three days after the prayer decision, and by the time of Schempp, another hundred had been offered. Some amendments directly attacked the Court's decisions; others provided for alternatives, such as voluntary prayer or a moment of silence; while some stipulated a more circuitous, dubious device of denying the federal courts jurisdiction in cases involving prayer.[48]

The congressional proposals produced several lengthy hearings. A wide spectrum of congressmen, religious denominations and organizations, and a variety of political action groups testified overwhelmingly in favor of some kind of amendment and some recognition of the right to religious expression as part of the American way of life. Much of the testimony, of course, was repetitious. Nevertheless, it offers a useful guide to the diverse reasons underlying the drive to reverse the Supreme Court's decisions.

1. *Prayer and allegiance to God are necessary weapons in the struggle against Communism*

For many Americans, the Cold War represented a struggle between the Satanic forces of atheistic Communism and those devoted to the glory of God, usually cast as Christians. In 1954, Congress officially enrolled the nation "under God" when it inserted that phrase in the Pledge of Allegiance. Senator Homer Ferguson (R-MI) summed up the congressional mood: "We know that America cannot be defended by guns, planes, and ships alone. Appropriations and expenditure for defense will be of value only if the God under whom we live believes that we are in the right. We should at all times recognize God's province over the lives of our people and over this great Nation."[49]

After the prayer decision, fundamentalist leader Dr. Carl McIntire complained that, given the "Communist conspiracy," the United States could not afford "to tamper with our dedication to God." A Louisiana congressman reminded his colleagues that the nation was "engaged in a life or death struggle with our mortal enemies of the Communist world." The Court's decisions, he said, made us no different from a Communist state. But, most important, we could not hope to win the Cold War "unless we are totally conscious that there is a God, . . . and that even the state is subject to His law." Numerous witnesses, including the national chaplain of the American Legion, reminded congressmen that Communism was the enemy, and lumped atheists and the

Supreme Court together as co-conspirators with Communists. Finally, the former Chancellor of the New York Board of Regents thought it imperative, given the "dangers of these difficult days" to teach children that God is their creator and that He has endowed them with their inalienable rights of life, liberty, and the pursuit of happiness.[50]

2. *Prayer is a vital weapon to combat social problems*

A schoolteacher and an activist in the National Committee to Revive School Prayer pointed to the appalling increase of social problems in the schools. She cited violence, dope addiction, theft, vandalism, truancy, arson, and even murder to demonstrate the nation's quickening moral and spiritual decay. She claimed that prayer offered mediation for troubled situations and provided some discipline. Others held secularism directly responsible for national social ills; those troubles, one witness claimed, were "nurtured by parents who do not stress sound religious values." She warned of severe consequences if we "deemphasized God" and if we stressed "with unrealistic minuteness the so-called historical distinctions between church and state." The Chasidic Lubavitcher Rabbi called for daily school prayers as a way to impress children that juvenile delinquency and wrongdoing was "an offense against the Divine Authority and order."

Some were concerned with adult delinquency as well. One congressman contended in 1964 that President Kennedy's assassination could not be divorced from the "lack of godliness that is being thrust upon us." The assassin, he argued, was a man without honor, conscience, or God. Unless American youths were exposed to religion, he warned, "we will raise other assassins, or a million assassins who will turn their backs on the Ten Commandments because they never heard them."[51]

3. *Prayer is the right of the majority*

The arguments here stressed the religiosity of the American people and the fact that "nearly everyone," as an Orthodox Rabbi stated it, believes in and worships God. Alabama Governor George Wallace demanded that Congress recognize "our rights"—presumably those of the majority. "We will not permit God and religion to be suppressed, outlawed, and banned," he warned. Others attacked the Court's decisions as "minority rights *ad absurdum*." The Florida Attorney General revealed typical anguish over the majority rule/minority rights tension: "I am not intimating that the majority is always right," he said, "but I do feel that the rights of the majority should not be infringed upon for the sake of satisfying a minority."

Representative John B. Anderson (R-IL), an active evangelical, who later ran for the presidency on an independent ticket in 1980, attempted to resolve that tension. In so doing, he, like others, sought to have pluralism embrace the minimum religious expression of faith in God. Ignoring any potential for coercion, Anderson argued that atheists—he expressed no concern for other minorities—had a right to be excused from prayer services. And this, he insisted, preserved both majority and minority rights, and thus maintained longstanding tradition. Finally, he argued that notwithstanding the practice of prayer and Bible-reading, the "pluralistic growth and development of American society had proceeded apace."[52] In short, officially-sponsored religiosity and pluralism were not incompatible.

4. *Prayer had been a vital part of the nation's traditions*

History, of course, has an advocacy purpose. During the long struggle over the prayer question, both sides regularly have turned to historical evidence to buttress their arguments. Prayer proponents, however, particularly relied on history to demonstrate that prayer and Bible-reading in the schools had been traditional and harmless. Such testimony is sprinkled with references to colonial religious origins, the religious passages of the Declaration of Independence, the invocations of divine faith at the Constitutional Convention, the words of Lincoln, prayer in Congress, and the expression, "God save this honorable Court," which opens every meeting of the Supreme Court. The lobbyist for the Women's Christian Temperance Union contended that "our forefathers and more immediate members of our families" fought and died to protect American liberties, including the right to pray in the schools. Another religious spokesman said that prayer maintained a state reliant upon God and not one of "secular materialism." A consistent theme throughout such testimony was that religious people, not atheists, founded their nation, and they "wisely" and "charitably" granted full freedom to all religions—even to atheists. That spirit allowed for the fullest expression of religious belief and must not, many insisted, be subverted.[53]

The congressional hearings reflected the mounting pressure and political activism of religious groups in American life. The extraordinary number of congressmen who testified during the various hearings indicates their recognition of that force. Any number of reasons possibly can explain the burgeoning religious activity. The cold war and nuclear anxieties, the transformation of the American economy with its resultant dislocations, the rootlessness associated with mass migrations, and the growing incidence of social problems such as alcoholism, drug addiction, divorce, and suicide, with their attendant external pressures on families, most readily come to mind.

The phenomenon of religiosity is not, of course, new; what is different in recent years is the emergence of a "religious right-wing" as a major political force in American life. The dramatic upsurge in evangelicalism and fundamentalism has accompanied active proselytizing, in both religion and politics. Joined with a political "New Right," we have "an alliance of mutual convenience" between the conservative religious community and the conservative political order. Richard Viguerie, the leading fundraiser for the "New Right," has targeted 100 million Americans—50 million born-again Protestants, 30 million "morally conservative" Catholics, 3 million Mormons, and 2 million Orthodox Jews—as the basis for a "pro-family, Bible-believing coalition."[54]

The political right in the United States consistently has wrapped itself in a religious mantle and argued that the international Communist conspiracy constituted a menace to western Christian civilization. Typically, the head of the John Birch Society declared that the struggle between Communism and Christianity would end with one side "completely triumphant and the other completely destroyed." Billy James Hargis, a prominent fundamentalist, once said that the nation must "choose Christ, for Christ loves America. Communism, which is of Satan, hates America."[55] Is it any wonder then that prayer—in any place—must be implemented to demonstrate that this is Christ's nation? While the Supreme Court no longer maintained that "this is a Christian nation," as it once did,[56] others thought differently: "Our forefathers were Christians," proclaimed one so-called patriotic group. "Has it come to pass that we must bow to the will of a mere handful of atheists and permit ourselves to become not only a pagan and unchristian nation, but a Communist welfare state?"[57]

The "electronic ministry," with its preachers and ministers adeptly exploiting television and radio, has provided the essential link for connecting political and religious conservatism. The Reverend Jerry Falwell, whose "Moral Majority" organization has emerged as the cutting edge for such views, broadcast over nearly four hundred television stations and three hundred radio stations. Falwell's "Top Secret Battle Plan for 1982" proposed pressures against television networks and advertizers to drop objectionable programs, opposition to homosexual equality, abortion, the ERA, pornography, the American Civil Liberties Union, and, of course, mobilization in behalf of the prayer amendment.[58]

Another group, the Crusade for Christ, largely financed by wealthy businessmen, raised over $30 million. The appeal again was blatantly politically conservative, with a religious, moral cover. In 1976, the director admitted that the CFC's purpose was to elect Christian conservatives. "Our vision," he said, "is to rebuild the foundations of the Republic as it was when first founded—a 'Christian Republic.' We must return to the faith of our fathers."[59]

Much of the current evangelical zeal in the United States—though certainly not all—reinforces and legitimates powerful strands of conservative political and social beliefs. The catalog of political and social goals serves an agenda for prophetic faith. The political evangelicals readily testify to their faith in a pluralistic America, but it is a *religiously* pluralistic society, not a secular one.[60]

Piety fulfills man's spiritual longings. The modern world is difficult. Traditional values have been assaulted on a number of fronts such as divorce, child custody arrangements, feminism, and abortion, to name the obvious. In turn, a rising cultural and moral relativism has led to an expanding preference for therapeutic, and not moral, solutions for personal happiness. Even religion, in the minds of some, has become too relativistic, too accommodating. As such, much of the current evangelical and fundamentalist fervor reflects a disenchanted response to "liberation theology," "modernism," and "secular humanism."

The dramatic increase in Christian schools illustrates the depth of dissatisfaction with "secular" society. One survey reported that three new Christian schools opened each day, and enrollment rose from 140,000 in 1971 to 450,000 in 1981. Racial desegregation and the prayer decision are often cited as the causes for growth. But the curricular concerns demonstrated much more. One school founder denounced the "creeping socialism" in the public schools, and noted that his school used McGuffey readers and taught the virtues of the gold standard, as decreed by biblical authority. He proudly said that "we espouse all the views of the Moral Majority and then some." A Virginia school director denounced the "humanistic flavor" of the public schools; for his children to return to those schools, he said, would be like the Israelis sending their children back to Egypt for school.

The political contents of these schools is apparent. A San Diego Christian schoolteacher was dismissed because he taught Emerson, Thoreau, and Shakespeare. He also opposed sending the band to a Reagan political rally; for this, he was given John Birch Society literature to better understand the school's political orientation.[61]

Two decades of protest against the Supreme Court's prayer ruling coalesced into a revived campaign for a constitutional amendment in the summer of 1983. President Reagan, flanked by the Reverend Falwell, announced his determination to secure such an amendment. The President originally had favored a simple statement providing "Nothing in this Constitution shall be construed to prohibit individual or group prayer in public schools or other public institutions. No person shall be required by the United States or any state to participate in prayer." Now, in an obvious effort to allay fears of governmental dictation, the president's proposal added: "Nor shall the United States or any state compose the words of any prayer to be said in public schools." A leading Senate supporter, Orrin Hatch (R-UT), suggested the addition but he urged the alternative of simply permitting silent prayer or meditation.[62]

Public support for the prayer amendment seemed sincere and well-grounded. Perhaps political and clerical leaders genuinely desire institutionalizing prayers in the schools. Nevertheless, whatever the intentions, the prayer issue perhaps has more utility as a cause for political agitation and activism than as an object of success. Senator Goldwater's *volte face* between 1964 and 1984 offers a preface to understanding the prayer issue largely as a manifestation of symbolic politics. The political manipulation of religious values also explains the dramatic difference between the responses of President Kennedy in 1962 and President Reagan in the early 1980s.

Symbolic politics serves a passive style of leadership that carefully avoids tough decisions "while at the same time posturing as a protagonist against an evanescent enemy," as Murray Edelman has written. While avoiding or deflecting real issues, political leaders maintain " 'symbolic leadership' through . . . publicized action on noncontroversial policies or on trivia, and through a dramaturgical performance emphasizing the traits popularly associated with leadership: forcefulness, responsibility, courage, decency, and so on."[63] Simply stated, the illusion of activity and leadership, expressed by manipulating symbols, conceals real passivity.

That, in no small measure, is Reagan's achievement. His attention to the prayer issue, particularly with the focused activity in the spring of 1984, reflects his attachment to symbolic politics. As he withdrew troops from Lebanon, in direct contradiction to reiterated guarantees that he would not, as he accumulated budget deficits that he always had excoriated as immoral and destructive, and as the jockeying for public favor and concern for imagery heightened in an election year, so his concern with the prayer issue increased. Image is so crucial and important, particularly to maintain faith in a morally complete leader, untainted by any deviation from conventional and traditional morality. Such an image is difficult to contest and almost irresistible.

"Reagan speaks for old values in current accents," a recent biographer has observed.[64] As such, those "old values" had a special currency as the prayer issue was debated in part as a symbolic act of vengeance on governmental and political policies antagonistic to the values that Reagan and his focused constituency share and treasure.

Several decades ago, historian Richard Hofstadter uncannily anticipated what has remained constant: "Ascetic Protestantism remains a significant undercurrent in contemporary America, and its . . . followers have found newfangled ways of reaffirming some of their convictions. They cannot bring back Prohibition or keep evolution entirely out of the schools. They have been unable even to defend school prayer or prevent *Life* magazine from featuring the topless bathing suit. But they can recriminate against the new America that outrages them, and they have found powerful leaders to echo their views."[65]

President Reagan has forcefully and eloquently echoed those views; indeed, he has shaped that kind of leadership into an art form. Public statements and articulated goals reflect not practical policies, but emotional and psychic needs. During the struggle for the prayer amendment in 1984, the President emphasized that the issue was one of his top three or four priorities. For example, when he announced his re-election campaign, he promised new efforts to create jobs, to control governmental spending, to keeping the peace, and finally to see "if we can't find room in our schools for God."[66]

Reagan's public statements have relied on equal doses of nationalism and patriotism, religious belief, and emotional exploitation. In an address specially devoted to the prayer issue, timed to match the opening of the Senate's debates, Reagan invoked the Mayflower Compact of 1620, the Declaration of Independence, the Pledge of Allegiance, the National Anthem, Benjamin

Franklin, and George Washington, all of which affirmed the role of God in the affairs of state. Given widespread Jewish opposition to schoolroom prayer, Reagan interestingly raised the issue of the Nazis' and Klan's right to march on public property and advocate the extermination of Jews, a right the courts had found protected by the First Amendment. Could that same amendment, he asked, forbid children from praying in schools? "Nonsense," he retorted; furthermore the proscription against prayer denied citizens of their "free exercise" right. "The pendulum has swung too far toward intolerance against genuine religious freedom. It's time to redress the balance," he concluded.[67] The President's analogy between demonstrating Nazis and the denial of prayer was commonplace. The rebuttal, of course, was obvious: one did not have to watch or listen to Nazis demonstrate; prayers in the schoolroom, however, voluntary or otherwise, carried a great potential for coercion.

Finally, the President insisted that his amendment called only for voluntary prayer, directly rejecting any notion that public officials might prescribe a common prayer. His simple aim, he emphasized, was to ensure that the "courts could not forbid our children from voluntary vocal prayer in their schools."[68] In a subsequent speech to religious broadcasters, President Reagan again insisted that his goals were minimal, but he could not resist casting the opposition as sinister and dangerous. He rejected any compromise that would have provided for a moment of silence in the classroom, flippantly noting that "we already have the right to remain silent—we can take the fifth amendment." The audience, perhaps equally dubious of Fifth Amendment guarantees, laughed.[69]

The speech to the broadcasters was pure symbolic politics. No schoolchild, of course, can be or is denied the right to pray voluntarily, as he or she wishes. Nevertheless the President found it useful to advocate what already exists and to raise evil straw men. The speech celebrated the Bible, attacked abortion, damned communism, criticized sexual promiscuity, drugs, and alcohol, and generally applauded the faith and aspirations of middle-class, white, Christian America. The beauty of symbolic politics is that the fulfillment of goals advanced and preached is almost beside the point; the persistent use of symbols is what counts. Make wheat deals, even an arrangement of arms control with the Soviets, but make certain to denounce the Soviets as untrustworthy and as the incarnation of evil; sign legislation expanding the scope of legalized abortion (as Reagan did as governor), but continue to preach against its wholesale use as "legalized murder"; denounce and threaten terrorists, yet rationalize the payment of ransom of hostages.[70] Similarly, the continued exploitation and manipulation of the prayer issue preempts virtue. Altogether the style is a proven recipe for American political success.

Events moved to a climax in March 1984 as the Senate prepared to vote on the proposed amendment. Lobbying intensified. Senators were deluged with mail, while pro-amendment forces beseiged the capitol with mass rallies, and all-night prayer vigils. The opposition seemed isolated, perhaps even over-whelmed. Nevertheless, several senators announced their determination to de-feat the measure. Significantly, some of the most outspoken opponents were from the President's party.

Senator Lowell Weicker (R-CT) largely focused on the constitutional ques-tion. He contended that voluntary prayer was not at issue, for any child had the right to pray. The amendment's real danger, he argued, was that it pro-posed some official organizational effort—whether it was a class, a school, or a law—to generate prayer; this, he believed, violated the dictates of the First Amendment. "Why forfeit our birthright of political liberty for a mess of spec-ulative, political pottage," he said.[71]

In addition, an impressive line-up of religious organizations urged the Sen-ate to reject the amendment using both constitutional and religious arguments. Senator John Danforth (R-MO), an ordained Episcopalian priest, eloquently spoke for those groups. Prayer, he said, was not meant to be mundane or trivial; instead, it was sacred and could not be diluted into something meaning-less to accommodate diversity.[72] Weicker's political concerns and Danforth's evangelical ones returned us full circle to the twin injunctions of Thomas Jeffer-son and Roger Williams.

The emotionalism generated by the issue inevitably led to loose, silly talk. Speaker Thomas O'Neill berated the President as a man who talked about prayer and yet did not go to church. Reverend Falwell immediately defended the President because he saved taxpayers hundreds of thousands of dollars by avoiding a security problem. A Republican congressman said that those "who favor a drug-ridden, pornographic, hedonistic society have every right to op-pose us." Pro-amendment spokesmen caustically noted that while the First Amendment did not specify "separation" of church and state, the Soviet Con-stitution actually contained such language.[73]

After several weeks of debate, on March 15, the Senate overwhelmingly rejected, 81-15, an amendment to permit silent prayers. Supporters of the pro-posal harshly criticized the President for failing to support it, hinting that he preferred to be defeated on his amendment for political reasons. The Presi-dent's motives, one senator said, were political and pointed toward the elec-tion: "President Reagan was not willing to really get a prayer amendment."

Five days later, by a 56-44 vote, 11 short of the necessary two-thirds major-ity, the Senate killed the President's proposal. Twenty-six Democrats and eighteen Republicans opposed the measure; only one southern Democrat voted against it, while the Republicans, excepting Goldwater and several oth-ers, all represented the party's moderate wing.

Reactions were predictable. Some Senate conservatives criticized the Presi-dent for delaying his lobbying activities; others believed that the Republican majority leader, Senator Howard Baker, only half-heartedly favored the mea-sure and merely sought favor for a future Presidential bid of his own. Falwell compained of "political oppression" and promised reprisals in the next elections.[74] In any event, for the seventh time since 1962, a serious effort to overturn the Supreme Court's ruling had failed. But there was no certainty that the issue was at an end; if anything, its symbolic value remained unimpaired, perhaps even enhanced.

The alliance of political conservatives with religious fundamentalists and evangelicals has raised profound concern for the stability of pluralist values. Indeed, the religious-political right has identified pluralism as evil itself—as the cause for "satanic churches," pornography, abortion, and demands for homosexual rights. "After the Christian majority takes control," one prominent leader has said, "pluralism will be seen as immoral and evil and the state will not permit anybody the right to practice evil." The Reverend Falwell is more oblique, but the message is largely the same: "I think we should be the moral conscience of a nation." But veteran evangelical leader Billy Graham admitted that the political-religious alliance disturbed him. "The hard right has no interest in religion except to manipulate it," Graham declared.[75]

For that alliance, the notion of a government neutral in religious affairs, free from religious influence, simply is unacceptable. The argument is neatly circular: neutrality is secularism and secularism is an unacceptable sectarian faith. Thus traditional pluralist arrangements, centering on neutrality, no longer are as viable. Are those arrangements to be altered? Must government accommodate and facilitate more religious practices and forms?

The Supreme Court's 1984 ruling narrowly upholding the right of a city to use public funds for displaying a nativity scene lends some support for that development. Chief Justice Burger's opinion equated Christianity and Americanism, largely on historical grounds, and gave a Christmas creche the same symbolic value as the flag. But as Justice Brennan argued in dissent, the use of religious symbols to celebrate Christmas is sectarian; as late as the mid-nineteenth century some Protestant denominations still regarded the holiday as "Popish." Interestingly, the Solicitor General of the United States joined with the mayor of Pawtucket, Rhode Island (in opposition to a Catholic plaintiff and the American Civil Liberties Union) in behalf of the city's display.[76] The federal government's active intervention and abandonment of neutrality fulfilled the demands of the political-religious right. In short, politics dictated constitutional postures.

Pluralism, as far as religion is concerned, refers to the multiple ways of believing and worshiping—or not believing and worshiping. The state is neutral; that is, it has no stake in whether or how people accept the idea of God, and no role in facilitating that belief. But the political-religious right insists on just such a role: *viz.* that the state has a stake in the business of God, while serenely believing that God has a special stake in the United States. This new version of pluralism actively solicits the use of the state in promoting religiosity, blithely believing we are now immune from the familiar consequences of such interference.

The nineteenth-century sectarian conflicts confirmed the desirability of governmental neutrality in religion in order to preserve social peace. Today, ironically, that position is under attack and is regarded by a substantial number of Americans as the source of social disharmony. It seems that neither historical texts, totems, nor experience are relevant for these disaffected political-social elements. Instead, they appeal to a vague, mystical religiosity, one that allegedly has operated throughout American history, a history divinely inspired and guided from colonial beginnings. What Robert Bellah has called American "civil religion" connects our national historical experiences with a divine afflatus and transcendent meaning.[77]

Religious values have a preeminent place in American political thought, law, and society—from the Puritan vision of a Zion in the wilderness, to the deism of some eighteenth-century political leaders, and to the meliorative social reforms of the twentieth century. Religious ideas need not remove themselves from political debate and public policymaking; indeed, religious institutions, leaders, and values are intimately involved in a wide range of policy issues. But the dividing line—the "wall of separation"—has a clear historical meaning. "From the standpoint of both history and of contemporary social reality," the Jesuit theologican John Courtney Murray has written, "the only tenable position is that the first two articles of the First Amendment are not articles of faith but articles of peace."[78] In short, Roger Williams' concern with the encroachment of the wilderness on the sanctity of the church gardens remains vital and relevant.

When unity is confused with uniformity, the delicate social peace of a pluralist society stands in jeopardy. The defeat of the prayer amendment in 1984 certainly did not mark an end to this threat.[79] Pro-prayer militants have promised to electorally punish their opponents and pursue their agenda. A well-organized, well-financed, politically conservative lobby finds religious concerns to be an effective catalyst for mobilization. Religion may or may not be the opiate of the masses in America; but apparently it is the adrenalin for a political activism that assaults the fragile bonds of pluralism, ironically in the cause of religious freedom.

University of Wisconsin

NOTES

*This essay is based on my Kenneth Keating Memorial Lecture, Tel Aviv University, 1984.

1. 370 U.S. 421 (1962). A year later, the Court struck down a Pennsylvania statute requiring daily Bible-reading sessions in the public schools, Abington School District v. Schempp, 374 U.S. 203 (1963).

2. Leonard W. Levy, *Judgments* (Chicago, 1972), 169-224. Levy recently summed up his own and other historical work on the origins of the Constitution's establishment clause, *The Establishment Clause: Religion and the First Amendment* (New York, 1986). The work sharply repudiates the recent attempts of former Chief Justice Burger's and now Chief Justice Rehnquist's attempts to impose a gloss on the First Amendment, arguing that Madison and other framers had no objection to non-preferential aid to religious groups. Also see Stanley I. Kutler, "How Shall We Sing the Lord's Song," *Present Tense* (January-February 1987); Thomas J. Curry, *The First Freedoms: Church and State in America to the Passage of the First Amendment* (New York, 1986).

3. *16 Writings of Thomas Jefferson* (1903), 281-282. See Leo Pfeffer, *Church, State, and Freedom* (Boston, 1953), for a typical celebration of Jefferson and Madison; Robert L. Cord, *Separation of Church and State: Historical Fact and Current Fiction* (New York, 1982), is more critical of Jefferson and Madison's inconsistencies. George Goldberg, *Reconsecrating America* (Grand Rapids, 1984), argues that twentieth-century standards of separation and anti-establishment violate the framer's original intentions. Levy, *Establishment Clause*, again has the upper hand, persuasively demonstrating that the original intention included opposition to non-preferential aid. Cf. Rehnquist, J., dissenting in Wallace v. Jaffree, 105 S. Ct. 2479 (1985).

4. Mark DeWolfe Howe, *The Garden and the Wilderness* (Chicago, 1965), 6-9. "The forces let loose by that revival still operated in 1790 to give the sanctity of the garden priority in the many minds over the prerogatives of the wilderness" (9).

5. Alexis de Tocqueville, *Democracy* (Vintage ed., New York, 1954), 1:310-324; 2:28.

6. Commonwealth v. Cooke, 7 Am. L. Reg. 417, 423 (1859); Howe, *Garden*, 93-99; Anson Phelps Stokes and Leo Pfeffer, *Church and State in the United States* (New York, 1964), 225-239.

7. Carl Kaestle, "Moral Education and Common Schools in America: A Historian's View," scheduled for publication in *Journal of Moral Education* (January 1985). Also see William Richard Adler, "Morals Education and Religious Freedom in Wisconsin: The Legal History of a Public Educational Problem" (LL.M. Thesis, University of Wisconsin Law School, 1982).

8. Stokes and Pfeffer, *Church and State*, 225-239; State ex rel Weiss v. Edgerton, 76 Wis. 177 (1890). Despite the clear lack of separation of church and state, David Dudley Field, a leader of the American bar and a notable legal theorist, confidently remarked that the "total and final separation" of church and state was the "greatest achievement of human progress." If this nation could boast of nothing else, he continued, "we could claim with justice that first among the nations we . . . made it an article of organic law that the relations between man and his maker were a private concern into which other men had no right to intrude," Field, "American Progress in Jurisprudence," *American Law Review*, 27 (1893): 645. The faith in separation clearly outstripped the reality. A few years earlier, James Bryce more perceptively commented that the national and state governments offered "Christianity a species of recognition inconsistent with the view that civil government should be absolutely neutral in religious matters," *The American Commonwealth*, 2 vols. (London, 1889), 2:560-561. A late nineteenth-century treatise on church-state relations noted that monogamy, the Christian Sabbath, and the public schools were institutions that "belong to both church and state" and had to be "main-

tained and regulated by both," Philip Schlaff, *Church and State in the United States* (1888), 69. A useful and new analysis of nineteenth-century church-state conflicts is Morton Borden, *Jews, Turks, and Infidels* (Chapel Hill, 1984).

9. Billard v. Board of Education of Topeka, 69 Kans. 53 (1904).

10. Kaestle, "Moral Education."

11. Cantwell v. Connecticut, 310 U.S. 296 (1940).

12. Everson v. Board of Education, 330 U.S. 1 (1947). Justice Rutledge, speaking for the dissenters, criticized Black's willingness to accept state aid for busing. The opinion was rooted in a more absolutist framework than Black's. Also see Jackson's biting, more personal dissent, taunting Black for his inconsistency.

13. McCollum v. Board of Education, 333 U.S. 203 (1948) [religious instruction on school grounds]; Zorach v. Clauson, 343 U.S. 306 (1952) [released time]; McGowan v. Maryland, 366 U.S. 420 (1962) [Sunday closing laws]; Sherbert v. Verner, 374 U.S. 398 (1963) [unemployment compensation].

14. 370 U.S. 421, 425 (1962).

15. Ibid., 427, 429, 436, 430.

16. Ibid., 430, 435.

17. 374 U.S. 203 (1963). See Justice Brennan's concurring opinion which offers an elaborate historical summary of the church-state problem, ibid., 230-304. Justice Potter dissented in both the prayer and Bible-reading cases, 370 U.S. 421, 444 (1962); 374 U.S. 203, 320 (9163).

18. *New York Times*, 28 June 1962.

19. Ibid., 26 June 1962. *Cong. Record*, 87 Cong., 2 Sess. (26 June 1962), 11775; (27 June 1962), 11844. Levy, *Judgments*, 226.

20. *Christian Century* (4 July 1962); 832; (11 July 1962), 856; (1 August 1962), 934. Cf. Board of Education v. Minor, 23 Oh. St. 211 (1872): "Legal Christianity is a solecism, a contradiction of terms. When Christianity asks the aid of government beyond mere impartial protection, it denies itself. Its laws are divine, and not human. Its essential interests lie beyond the reach and range of human government. United with government, religion never rises above the merest superstition; united with religion, government never rises above the merest despotism; and all history shows us that the more widely and completely they are separated, the better it is for both."

21. *Commonweal* (13 July 1962), 387.

22. *Catholic World* (August 1962), 265; *America* (7 July 1962), 456.

23. Ibid. (1 September 1962), 665-666; (28 July 1962), 541.

24. Levy, *Judgments*, 225-233.

25. *America* (8 September 1962), 679-680; *National Review* (11 September 1962).

26. *New York Times*, 2 July 1962.

27. My comments on polling derive from a reading of all post-World War II Gallup polls concerning religious faith and practice.

28. Engel v. Vitale, 370 U.S. 421, 435, 440n; Abington School District v. Schempp. 374 U.S. 203, 230-304 (Brennan's concurring opinion).

29. *Cong. Record*, 87 Cong., 2 Sess. (27 Sept. 1962) 21100-02; *ibid.*, (4 Oct. 1962), 22274-75. Bernard Schwartz, *Super Chief: Earl Warren and His Supreme Court* (unabridged edition, New York, 1983), 468.

30. Jonathan Martin Kolkey, *The New Right, 1960-1968, With Epilogue, 1969-1980* (Washington, 1983), 103. Buckley's *National Review* earlier had pressed Goldwater to denounce the prayer decision, 19 May 1964, 406.

31. Everson v. Board of Education, 330 U.S. 1 (1947); Zorach v. Clauson, 343 U.S. 306 (1952); McGowan v. Maryland, 366 U.S. 420 (1961). Levy, *Judgments*, 232-233.

32. 403 U.S. 602 (1971).

33. Ring v. Grand Forks Public School District, 483 F. Supp. 272 (D. ND 1980).

34. Lemon v. Kurtzman, 403 U.S. 602 (1970).

35. Committee for Public Education and Religious Liberty v. Nyquist, 413 U.S. 746 (1972); Hunt v. McNair, 413 U.S. 734 (1972).

36. Fink v. Board of Education of Warren Co., 442 A 2d 837 (Pa. Common Ct. 1982); Lynch v. Indiana State University Board of Trustees, 378 N.E. 2d 900 (Ind. Ct. App. 1978).

37. Doe v. Aldine School Dist., 563 F. Supp. 883 (S.D. Tex. 1982).

38. On voluntary prayer, see, for example, Kent v. Commissioner of Education, 402 N.E. 2d 1340 (Mass. 1980; Karen B. v. Treen, 653 F. 2d 897 (5th Cir. 1981); Stein v. Oshinsky, 348 F. 2d 999 (2d Circ. 1965); DeSpain v. DeKalb Co. Community School District, 384 F. 2d 836 (7th Cir. 1967); for Bible-reading, see Mangold v. Gallatin School Dist., 438 F. 2d 1194 (3rd Cir. 1971); Meltzer v. Bd. of Public Instruction, 548 F. 2d 573 (5th Cir. 1977); Jones v. Allen, 231 F. Supp. 852 (D. Del. 1964).

39. Beck v. McElrath, 548 F. Supp., 1161 (M.D. Tenn. 1982); May v. Cooperman (D. N.J., 24 October 1983). But cf. Gaines v. Anderson, 421 F. Supp. 337 (D. Mass. 1976). On 2 April 1984, voters in Framingham, Massachusetts narrowly defeated a referendum calling for voluntary school prayers based on the Declaration of Independence. A good analysis of the moment of silence issue is in "Daily Moments of Silence in Public Schools: A Constitutional Analysis," *New York University New Review*, 58 (1983); 364-408. But the issue remains quite vital. See note 79, *infra*.

40. See Justice Rehnquist's dissent in Stone v. Graham, 449 U.S. 39, 43 (1980).

41. DeSpain v. DeKalb Co. Community School District, 384 F. 2d 836 (7th Cir. 1967).

42. Grasberg v. Devebio, 380 F. Supp. 285 (E.D. Va. 1974); Wood v. Mt. Lebanon School Dist., 342 F. Supp. 1293 (W.D. Pa. 1972).

43. Smith v. Denny, 280 F. Supp. 651 (E.D. Cal. 1968).

44. O'Hair v. Paine, 312 F. Supp. 434 (W.D. Tex. 1969).

45. O'Hair v. Paine, 432 F. 2d 66 (5th Cir. 1970).

46. Aronow v. U.S., 432 F. 2d 242 (9th Cir. 1970).

47. Zorach v. Clauson, 343 U.S. 306, 313-314 (1952).

48. David M. Ackerman, "Legal Analysis of President Reagan's Proposed Constitutional Amendment on School Prayer" (Congressional Research Service, Library of Congress, 1982), 22.

49. *Cong. Record*, 83 Cong., 2 Sess., 6348.

50. *Proposed Amendments to the Constitution Relating to Prayers and Bible Reading in the Public Schools*, Committee on the Judiciary, House of Representatives, 88 Cong., 2 Sess. (13 May 1964), 1517; (22 April 1964), 506; (6 May 1964), 1075, 1107; (29 April 1964), 634.

51. Rebbe M. Schneerson [Lubavitcher Rabbi], "A Petition for G-D," (Brooklyn, 1983). *Prayer in the Public Schools and Buildings*, Subcommittee on Courts, Civil Liberties, and the Administration of Justice of the Committee on the Judiciary, House of Representatives, 96 Cong., 2 Sess. (9 September 1980), 496-497; *Proposed Amendments*, note 50 *supra* (7 May 1964), 1212, 1228.

52. Ibid., (22 April 1964), 219; (29 April 1964), 855, 639; (23 April 1964), 387; (20 May 1964), 1855; (22 April 1964), 321.

53. Ibid., (6 May 1964), 1168; (7 May 1964), 1307-1308; (8 May 1964), 1392; (23 April 1964), 528; *Prayer in Public Schools*, note 51 *supra* (30 July 1980), 189.

54. John S. Saloma III, *Ominous Politics: The New Conservative Labyrinth* (New York, 1984), 52-60. Booth Fowler, *A New Engagement: Evangelical Political Thought, 1966-1976* (Grand Rapids, 1982) ably argues that evangelicism is not exclusively linked to right-wing politics. George Marsden, *Fundamentalism and American Culture* (New York, 1980), traces the evangelical/fundamentalist revolt against the social gospel and toward the pursuit of individual salvation and repentance. But, as Fowler demonstrates, numerous modern evangelicals are committed to social reform, albeit with a different emphasis than their early twentieth-century predecessors, Fowler, *A New Engagement*, 169.

55. Kolkey, *New Right*, 78, 79.

56. Church of the Holy Trinity v. United States, 143 U.S. 457, 471 (1892).

57. *Sons of the American Revolution Magazine* (October 1963), 1.

58. Saloma, *Ominous Politics*, 58.

59. Ibid., 54. Flo Conway and Jim Siegelman, *Holy Terror: The Fundamentalist War on America's Freedoms* (New York, 1982).

60. Fowler, *A New Engagement*.

61. *Time* (8 June 1981), 54-56.

62. *New York Times*, 13 July 1983.

63. Murray Edelman, *The Symbolic Uses of Politics* (Urbana, 1964), 81.

64. Robert Dallek, *Ronald Reagan: The Politics of Symbolism* (Cambridge, 1984), 3.

65. Richard Hofstadter, *The Paranoid Style in American Politics and Other Essays* (New York, 1965), 77-80.

66. *Weekly Compilation of Presidential Documents* (29 January 1984); ibid., (22 February 1984).

67. Ibid. (25 February, 1984).

68. Ibid.

69. Ibid., (30 January 1984).

70. Dallek, *Reagan*, passim.

71. *New York Times*, 16 March 1984, 21 March 1984.

72. *Cong. Record*, 98 Cong., 2 Sess. (5 March 1984), 2345-2347.

73. *Milwaukee Journal*, 11 March 1984.

74. *New York Times*, 21 March 1984. President Reagan repeatedly made it clear that he would continue his fight and again attempted to preempt the field of religious virtue. Following his renomination in August 1984, he told a prayer breakfast in Dallas: "We establish no religion in this country, nor will we ever. We command no worship. We mandate no belief. But we poison our society when we remove its theological underpinnings. We court corruption when we leave it bereft of belief," *New York Times*, 24 August 1984.

75. Saloma, *Ominous Politics*, 59-60. The most recent work on politics and the religious right is Gillian Peele, *Revival & Reaction: The Right in Contemporary America* (Oxford, 1984).

76. Lynch v. Donnelly, U.S. Law Week (5 March, 1984) 4317-4324. Also see Justice Brennan's dissent, ibid., 4325-4333. Interestingly, pro-prayer conservative columnist James J. Kilpatrick vigorously attacked the creche decision. '[T]he government has no business promoting the divinity of Jesus Christ," he wrote, *Milwaukee Journal*, 2 December 1984. For many, the Court's 1983 decision in Marsh v. Chambers, approving the Nebraska legislature's hiring of clergy for daily prayers, similarly constituted a retreat from the line of cases from Engel to Lemon. But here the Court relied heavily on deeply-established historical tradition. Furthermore, it could be argued that the Nebraska cases involved adults, who were ostensibly better prepared to resist improper religious indoctrination. 103 S. Ct. 330 (1983).

77. Robert N. Bellah, "Civil Religion in America," in Russell E. Richey and Donald G. Jones, eds., *American Civil Religion* (New York, 1974). Lincoln's Second Inaugural Address and Kennedy's Inaugural Address offer clear illustrations of the divine strains in civil religion. But see Brennan's dissent in Lynch v. Donnelly, note 76 *supra*, for a comment on the meaninglessness of many religious incantations. Also see Charles Krauthammer, "America's Holy War," *The New Republic* (9 April 1984), 15-18.

78. John Courtney Murray, S.J., *We Hold These Truths: Catholic Reflections on the American Proposition* (New York, 1960). Also see Paul G. Kauper, *Religion and the Constitution* (Baton Rouge, 1964), 83. Religious institutions, Kauper said, "transgress their proper function when they attempt to impose their own peculiar moral beliefs derived from religious insight upon others who do not share these beliefs and insights." Opponents of the religious right occasionally forget what many of them would regard as the socially useful role of religious groups in the civil rights and anti-Viet Nam war movements. For an example of a reasoned plea for more recognition of religion as part of pluralism, see Richard John Neuhaus, *The Naked Public Square* (Grand Rapids, 1984). For Neuhaus, the cultural, political, and legal crisis is attributable to the fact that "the popularly accessible and vibrant belief systems and world views of our society are largely excluded from the public arena in which the decisions are made about how the society should be ordered," 258-259. Cf. Michael E. Smith, "The Special Place of Religion in the Constitution," *Supreme Court Review* (Chicago, 1983), 83-124.

79. See Wallace v. Jaffree, 105 S. Ct. 2479 (1985) where the Court, by a 6-3 vote, invali-
dated an Alabama law that authorized a moment of silence "for meditation" in the
public schools. The majority found that the statute clearly had a religious intent. It is
instructive to compare Justice Rehnquist's historical excursion in dissent with Levy's,
The Establishment Clause. Many local school districts, essentially homogeneous, regularly have defied the Court's ban on school prayers, see *The Wall Street Journal*, 5
March 1984. We have a substantial body of literature from the 1960s and 1970s, assess-
ing the impact of the Court's prayer decision, see, e.g., William K. Muir, Jr., *Prayer in
the Public Schools: Law and Attitude Change* (Chicago, 1967); Kenneth M. Dolbeare
and Philip E. Hammond, *The School Prayer Decisions: From Court Policy to Local
Practice* (Chicago, 1971).